How to be Zen in a Crisis

ALSO BY SAMANTHA GORDON

How to be Zen in a Crisis Journal

SAMBAE ZEN ONLINE

Amazon.com/author/sambaezen

Instagram: @sambaezen

Facebook.com/sambaezen

Twitter.com/sambaezen

How to be Zen in a Crisis

A practical guide for surviving and thriving during life's catastrophes and even a pandemic

Samantha Gordon

A Sambae Zen Book

Copyright © 2020 by Samantha Gordon
A Sambae Zen book
Published on Amazon

Graphic Design: Samantha Gordon
Cover Design: Samantha Gordon
Editorial: Samantha Gordon
Author Photo: Karolina Turek

All rights reserved. This book may not be reproduced in whole or in part without written permission from the author, except by a reviewer who may quote brief passages in a review; nor may any part of this book be reproduced, stored in a retrieval system, or transmitted in any form or by any means, electronic, mechanical, photocopying, recording, or other, without written permission from the author.

Note: The term "zen" is not meant to convey any Buddhist religious overtones from the noun Zen; it is merely used as a colloquial adjective to describe the state of peace.

To the world in crisis,
we're all in this together

Contents

Introduction 11
You are in a crisis......................................15
Detach from the crisis..............................28
Assess the truth and the non-truths........41
Strategize 50
Anxiety is not the answer.........................57
Keep moving forward 64
Know yourself, know reality, know who you're dealing with 68
Understand it's not personal 74
Feel everything...77
Know it was bound to happen 84
One at a time..87
Welcome moral support..........................91
Take care of your vessel 99
Harness your energy 107
Forgive all...111
Give up the outcome 117
Learn the lesson 121
Laugh Laugh Laugh................................131
Focus on what matters 135
Be patient 138
Start afresh 142
Feel the gratitude...................................146
Embrace the zen....................................151

Be zen and be zen again 164
Acknowledgements..170

May I become at all times...
A protector for those
without protection
A guide for those who have
lost their way

DALAI LAMA

Introduction

To be in a crisis, according to Cambridge Dictionary:

-experiencing a time of great difficulty, danger or suffering.

Crises have a way of jumping out at us. You're going about your life and then one day, probably not on day one, you realize it has started. You weren't ready in some way shape or form and now it's here.

You're in a crisis.

Your world is off kilter and your prefrontal cortex is firing at wrong times, in wrong ways, causing you to make ill-conceived decisions based on poor anticipatory event diagnostics. In other words, you are somewhere between losing your mind and going cuckoo bananas.
Something needs to get better and the first thing is you.

Your number one priority now is to get zen. What is zen, in this context, and why do we want to be it?

zen - adjective

-relaxed and not worrying about things you cannot change.

Synonyms [with my own additions]:

cool as a [motherloving] cucumber

calm [af]

relaxed [as shit]

unruffled [come at me bruh]

Why?

Our survival depends on it.

Being zen, has a fundamental role in shaping our brain, whereby it can better assist us through a crisis. Numerous studies have shown that relaxation techniques, being mindful and being zen can allow us to not only be more relaxed, but to have better awareness of what is happening around us and improve our decision making capabilities.

We aren't trying to get zen because it's in vogue.

We aren't trying to get zen because we think people will think we're cool.

We aren't trying to get zen to impress someone.

We aren't trying to get zen because we look really great in yoga pants (but I mean, props to you if you do).

We are getting zen because it is essential.

And since we are in a crisis, it is as difficult as ever and as *crucial* as ever.

Once you have yourself centered, the benefits are far reaching. You are able to make good decisions from a clear mindset, and therefore, be protected, peaceful and happy. You not only survive the crisis but thrive in it and from it. Your life will be forever improved by it, instead of crippled from the experience.

You can be calm in the middle of the storm. You can be a pillar of peace in a hurricane. Let's find the eye of the storm. Let's be the eye of the storm until it dissipates.

We have no time to waste, so let's get to it.

> There cannot be a crisis next week. My schedule is already full.
>
> — HENRY KISSINGER

You are in a crisis

We don't all come out of the womb, in the lotus position singing soprano opera in meditative bliss. That being said, a very good self-development yogi with their head on straight (or their head upside down in a handstand) knows how to clear their mind on a normal day with normal stressors. A usually centered person can even clear their head on a day when things are a bit more intense... but what about when shit absolutely hits the fan?

I am talking about those situations that we all face in life, whether they be a global pandemic (*ahem*), a bad boss who is sexually harassing you, rape, court cases, breakups, divorces, kidnaps, deaths, injuries, sickness, sociopaths reeking havoc in your life, a combination of many or any sort of other impending doom... real crisis comes in many forms. It doesn't matter which particular flavour of crisis you are experiencing; they all have a similar vein of terror and panic that runs through them.

I am talking about those real crises we all face at some point in our lives, whether we think we are immune to them or not (that was a covid pun - too soon?).

Can we find our zen in the middle of a crisis and not only survive but come out better than ever and full of peace?

Yes, yes we can.

Let's get down to basics since you're probably in the midst of a crisis and we need to break it down simply and efficiently.

Who? You.

Where? Your crisis location here.

What? Turning your crisis into a zen point of power, where you are in control of your emotions, make the wisest decisions based on the information provided and enjoy yourself in the process.

Why? Your sanity and life depends on it (possibly others as well).

When? Now.

How? Well, let's start at the beginning.

Maybe you feel like you're living in a doom's day movie where you are either the protagonist of the story or one of the first nameless people to die, and you aren't sure which yet. There's a war happening - either with weapons or on your health.

Whatever it is, something diabolical is happening. You are being attacked in some way shape or form. You've gone through, or are still going through, a full blown crisis. There's probably shifting dynamics, your world seems to be lit aflame and for whatever reason, this is the most stressful time of your life.

Maybe, just maybe, you're in the middle of a global pandemic and are scared to hear a cough, the grocery shelves are barren, the city is shut down and you've lost your job. Maybe you used to do yoga and shop at Lululemon, and both are now boarded up to the ceiling. Maybe the stores have reopened but everything is still wack to the exponent of 1000.

It really doesn't matter, the point is - SHIT HAS HIT THE FAN. Shit has hit the fan more than it has ever hit the fan, more than you knew shit could hit the fan. You didn't know shit could smell so foul or that it could spread so wide. You are drowning in shit and it is hitting your face at circadian intervals. WELCOME TO THE CRISIS.

Maybe you are knee or neck deep in a crisis or perhaps you aren't anywhere near a crisis… yet.

Yet?!? You cry.

Yes, *yet*. You *will* have a crisis if you haven't already. Life gets us all. Duh duh dunnnnn.

Just teasing, no duh duh dun. It is more of a "Ah right, here it is, the trying time of our lives we all have to face at some point or other."

The point is, you know you're in it now so now you can get through it.

You must know thee are in a crisis, to get through thy crisis.

Fun fact: Crises do happen to everyone in some form or another (and always have throughout time). People can survive and thrive during and after a crisis *if* they make the right decisions and have the right headspace to do so, aka they get zen.

Don't wait until you're in a crisis to come up with a crisis plan.
-Dr. Phil McGraw

(But don't freak out if you're already in the crisis - better late than never to know it, my friend… we'll get back to that in a second.)

If you are prepared and can spot a crisis before you even enter it (or are early on in the game), you are well ahead of the curve. You can avoid all or most of the nasty side effects of being blindsided and unprepared. In fact, even if you are well into the storm (and have even gone past the first wave of a spiking coronavirus curve), you can still be calm and collected from this point on.

Imagine seeing the storm and knowing you have a bomb shelter - not just a bomb shelter but a NORAD early warning system to detect storms before they are even brewing. You can protect yourself and make the best decisions from a point of peace.

First things first, are you really in a crisis or are you just a hot mess in hot pants?

Sometimes it can be difficult to assess, since if you are in a bona fide crisis, you probably don't have your normal mental facilities about you. Also, you may be in denial, because you don't want anything to be wrong, and you want to believe everything's peachy.

Here are some signs you are in a crisis (but you are telling yourself it's fine as your world goes up in flames) vs. signs you *aren't* in a crisis and you are the one starting imaginary fires:

Signs you're in a bona fide crisis	Signs your issue is more internal than external
You are experiencing a global pandemic or massive community emergency.	You create emergencies when you're feeling bored.
You are in a situation that could have, should have or does have lawyers involved.	You are in a situation that your friends and family members are rolling their eyes at; they are sick of hearing you talk about something that you shouldn't be stressing over.
One or many of your	None of your human

human rights are being violated.	rights are being violated and you can't justify your extreme reactions.
You never considered yourself a stressed out person but you are suddenly in a constant state of stress due to your external environment (but nothing is due to your external environment... Eckhart Tolle, calm down, the message here is that someone or something is violating you in some real way... virus, war, abuse, court, harassment, verbal, physical, sexual, wildfire, etc.).	You are anxious for no reason; you are the crisis.
You feel like you're in a horror film and are the victim. Jaws music plays indefinitely in the background because you are always in imminent danger. It doesn't matter if the	You suspect deep down, you just need some fresh air and some perspective.

antagonist wears a suit or pencil skirt, is a giant cloud of insects or an infectious disease causing rampage, it is coming for you.	
Your heart rate on your fancy technology watch, or the heart rate monitor on the cardio machine at the gym, gives constant warnings that you are exceeding the limits of healthy heart functioning.	You've been solely engaging in negative self-talk and are creating your own spiral.
Your intuition and all of your external circumstances are screaming you're in a crisis!	Your intuition *always* tells you… you're a bit neurotic and you probably just need to get out of your own head.
Your child's pose is just you rocking back and forth, weeping.	You are a big baby.
You've stopped doing yoga and stopped meditating… and stopped sleeping and stopped remembering	Objectively, nothing that bad is really happening, it's just the story you're telling yourself. It's

to breathe from time to time and gasp for air suddenly and reach for books on how to get out of a crisis and to a place of zen but really you'd settle for just being OK...! *gasp*	hard to admit but you are realizing you may be your own problem.

The truth is, true shit can be all consuming to the point of crippling effects and even when we have practiced yoga and/or meditation for a while, there are some events in life that can shake us to the core with overwhelming anxiety and fear.

You can't think of anything else. You try to sleep but can't. Maybe you sleep for two hours and then shoot up two hours later consumed with panic. It is those moments when no number of handstands are going to put your head back on straight. So how do you get from the stress of a crisis (even while you're still in a crisis) to a point of zen?

Sometimes your beginning is not the true beginning of the crisis. This is fine, if not totally expected, as how should you know shit was hitting the fan until it was swirling around the room, putridly pungent in the air and hitting you in the face?

Where are you in the crisis?

Find which stage you are at in the stress to zen evolution. Many only acknowledge they are in a crisis at the last moment, but perhaps you found it much earlier and can potentially skip some steps.

The Stages of Stress to Zen:

1. Oh shit something's happening that is really, really messed up
2. Shock, paralyzed fear
3. Oh my goodness... it's worse than previously thought
4. The sleepless nights begin
5. Pure panic
6. Needy as hell (you start calling your mom too much) or you start running away from your loved ones and barking at them when they come near
7. You start needing to hydrate a lot more because your eyeballs have become waterfalls and you never were especially emotional to begin with
8. If you normally are super emotional, then add another step of manic crying, maybe manic yell-crying (whatever flavour of crying is your favourite when you're losing your mind)
9. Calm before the other storm, you're in denial
10. Head-spinning panic, you should have seen this coming but you didn't (also someone probably betrayed you... this is a crisis after all)

11. Shitting your pants and shaving your head
12. You start to lose the will to live and all energy has been sucked from your very soul
13. If you were religious before, you think God has forsaken you. If you were an atheist before, you start praying to a God you don't believe in. You possibly oscillate between both. You take up Buddhism but also do the Catholic rosary and start eating Kosher (to cover all the bases).
14. Nothing matters anymore, including the situation (you've somewhat embraced nihilism but in a non-suicidal way)
15. You come to accept something needs to change or else you're going to completely lose everything, including your mind
16. **You read "How to Be Zen in a Crisis" and do the inner work**
17. You have mastered the worst of it and are now invincible - you are the power of now, Eckhart Tolle calls you for advice

Now, you may not even be aware you are in each state until you have reached the solving stage. Most people are in denial for a long time, or living in a state of delusion, where crises don't happen to good people who meditate and do yoga regularly. Oh, but they do, so let's be prepared. If you are already in one, buckle up and let's find our zen.

Let's take this moment now to acknowledge where we are and the reality of the crisis.

Let's also take the time to acknowledge the situation for what it is (not worse or better than it is). We may only scratch the surface at this stage but we are starting to lay the foundation for healing from the ground up.

You will survive (at the very least). This zen journey will allow you to claim control of your mind and emotional state when you can't control your outer surroundings. You will center yourself so you can accurately assess what is happening and take steps to come out of it. One day you will see this experience as a rewarding challenge that gave you the confidence to be impenetrable. You will have faced, and made it through, the worst of it. This is your journey to conquer.

Spoiler alert: you will come out stronger in the end if you don't go completely bat shit crazy. Also, surprise, if you did feel a little bat shit crazy already, you still can make it out all right in the end! Take another look at that crisis to zen evolution list... you're well on track. A couple near meltdowns in the midst of a crisis are par for the course really, it is just how you bounce back after that makes all the difference.

If we can avoid a meltdown, fantastic (and you will mitigate that risk after using these tools) but know that if you've already had one, NO BIG DEAL. In fact, I'm surprised you didn't have more after what you are going through. You mean you're still breathing after all that? You mean, you didn't rip all your clothes off and go running through the streets screaming obscenities because you feel powerless to the crisis?

Congratulations!

So let's give this zen process a go since your crisis is not really working for you up until now, is it?

Good, let's get this show on the road…

Our biggest takeaway: accept you are in a crisis.

Attachment is the great fabricator of illusions; reality can be obtained only by someone who is detached.

SIMONE WEIL

Detach from the crisis

Always know when to leave the circus.

There's a solid chance you are pushed to your limit already and are neck deep in it, struggling to get out. Having a crisis is scary. Let's try to lessen the effects first so that we can look at it objectively. You're in enough of a traumatic experience, let's for a moment, liken the crisis to a circus.

the crisis = the circus

Ah, the circus. Lots of bizarre things are occuring. There's a ring of fire, painted faces and wild animals doing strange things.

Lucky for you, you know you are in the circus now. You see the zoo animals (maybe not all of them) but at least you are aware you are in the circus tent. Maybe you weren't aware that you were in the circus tent until now and wish you knew sooner, but the point is you know you're in it now.

Don't beat yourself up about it - crises have a way of sneaking up on you in a way where you look back and think *but it is so obvious looking back!!!* The writing wasn't just on the wall but it may have been written across the sky.

Sometimes we're not aware we're in the circus until we are well into the circus, many shows in, and in the lion's cage.

The lion may be gnawing on your left ankle, when you finally concede that maybe the situation was indeed serious and no it wouldn't just magically disappear if you acted as if nothing messed up was happening. No, it wasn't just a nice kitty coming up to be pet.

Let's take the situation of a pandemic. For those of whom took heed to the expert information in other places, before there was an emergency in your own area, you didn't know if you were overreacting. How would you know for sure if the virus would spread to your area. You'd never lived through a pandemic, and all of your friends were going about their lives as usual, not realizing that the entire world would be turned upside down in a week.

Chaos and predicaments have a way of happening fast. Maybe you were the friend with the lack of information, maybe it all hit you when the government locked down your city. Whether you suspected a shitstorm was brewing or not - you weren't sure before. Now you know.

So be thankful to have the peace of mind of actually knowing your situation as it is now. We know we're in the circus so let's get out. You have just enough information to make the next right decision.

That is such a position of power to know you are in a tutu in the circus. Of course you don't want to be there, but it is imperative to know you are in a tutu before you try to get out of it and escape the circus.

And you may not have all of the details of the type of circus you are in - how many shows? Will there be an encore? Will the encore be even crazier? Will you wear this itchy tutu the whole time or will there be a change of wardrobe? What sort of characters will be showing up? Will they be the same as before or different? Will they all be wearing masks? Will the lions eat the masks before we can wear the masks? These are all details that don't matter right now. Right now we are just dealing with what is, right now.

No matter what time you are reading this, the time is right now o'clock.

Regardless of how ahead of the game you were, we can't go back in time to change things, so let's do what we can from now on. That would be both very practical AND very zen of us to embrace the present moment.

Ommm? Yes.

Ok, so you're in the circus tent. The clowns are in the corner with inconspicuous facial contortions. You're aware you're in a crisis so it is time to get out *if safe to do so*.

Yes, physically remove yourself from the toxic environment if possible.

Leave the circus, pack your stuff and make a quiet exit stage left. If you know shit is about to hit the fan or it has already hit the fan - you are in danger. Remove yourself from imminent danger.

Now, you don't need to run. I mean, sometimes you need to run, if you're in the sort of crisis that requires running. I think you'll know in the moment and by golly, I hope you've been training for it. But no, for most crises, at most it's a speed walking tempo, maybe a light jog, but again, if you've forgotten your sports bra then nevermind, speed walking as previously said. The point is to put one foot in front of the other, with or without lifting the heel (or whatever the rule is to qualify for speed walking at the olympics).

Don't wait until things have escalated past the point of no return. Don't wait to see if it gets worse.

We've already determined it is a crisis. It's like those signs on the fire escape that tell you not to panic and make your way to your nearest exit. It doesn't mean you sit there and contemplate life's complexities as you stare at the exit map in a state of denial - no, just get going.

Be zen, don't be silly.

It's time to leave the circus and accept the lions aren't kitties.

An example of this is experiencing a pandemic. We take the necessary precautions to protect ourselves and the community at large from a deadly virus. We wash our hands, we social distance, we trade our fancy pants for our comfy pants or no pants at home. We remove ourselves from public contamination as much as possible in order to save ourselves and others.

If we absolutely must go out in the world, then we both limit our exposure, and prevent the spread by following the recommended guidelines of epidemiologists and public health professionals (and not the neighbour next door whose cat told him it was OK to go to a party). Cats are liars who just want the house to themselves.

BUT! There's a caveat to removing yourself from the toxic situation immediately. Sometimes it isn't possible to leave the crisis or it is not in your long-term best interest to leave in the present state. This can be true for many situations.

Quite often you need a game plan while staying in the circus, before you can tame the tiger and ride out of the circus tent.

You need a map, you need to plan where you're going when you leave the circus and most importantly, you need to make sure you are

SAFE to leave. Sometimes you have to keep your enemies close (maybe just for a little bit longer) so you can prepare yourself effectively to make the leap.

It is possible you need to plan your escape route, for whatever reason, to mitigate damage. Of course this is a risk but sometimes you must stay in the toxic environment to win in the end. Winning may mean hanging in there and staying mentally strong - sometimes there isn't much of a choice and you do what you have to do, even when you'd love to leave immediately.

Times it pays off to stay in the toxic environment for a touch longer:

1. Your life isn't immediately threatened and your long-term gain far exceeds the temporary pain and discomfort you may be presented with in the interim.

2. You know in your heart/gut/deep logical reasoning that lining up your ducks will be beneficial.

For example, this may be planning your escape from an abusive live-in relationship that isn't life threatening, sticking in there for a court case, or anything else that has major benefits for yourself and others (directly or remotely involved).

Sometimes we have to face things for the better of all. There is such a thing as precedence in court cases. That means if you stick it out and fight for what's right, all those cases after you will look to your case and it will support their win. Yes, truly. So it may look like you're just sticking up for yourself but in reality, you are laying the foundation of strength for those who fall into the same predicament in the future. Your fight and your win can mean more than you will ever know.

And maybe it isn't a court case, perhaps it is just a story of survival and one friend of a friend hears it and finds the strength to survive too. Your magnitude can sweep in so many wonderful ways, so don't give up. Yes, it's hard. It's a crisis. That's to be expected.

In the example of a pandemic, perhaps you are an essential worker in a high risk job. Maybe you are a doctor or nurse working on the frontlines facing the crisis everyday. You are in it and your service is vital. It is in your best interest, and the community's best interest, to stay in the heat of the battle.

If you're staying in it for the long-term benefit, what does this mean?

If boundaries are not withheld outside of your body, you have to enforce them within.

When you are in a state of absolute chaos and terror, you must detach from it so you can see clearly.

You need to clear your inner environment.

You can call it a host of things: meditation, getting centered or finding your inner zen.

You need to clear your inner environment both if you can't leave the situation AND if you have left the situation (temporarily or for good). Either way, you need to get the crisis out of your system internally. It is especially important for those still in the trenches.

If you can't remove yourself from the toxic environment outside, then remove yourself from the toxic environment inside (if only in moments). How? Detach from the crisis.

Meditative exercises

For those who have a strong practice of meditation, this may be easier for you - or it may not be, because the crisis has flipped you up, thrown you on the pavement and broken your meditation bones. Either way, let's make our way from here.

Meditation comes in many forms. The type of meditation you practice is less important than the final peaceful result.

As a general whole, the idea is to move your mind from a scattered and fearful place to a place of peaceful awareness. That may come through observing your breath, repeating a mantra, simply accepting your beingness as you are, or any number of meditation types.

The types within this book are guided meditations for you to follow, which can cater to both beginners and advanced practitioners of meditation. These written guided meditative exercises, provided throughout this book, are a great way to start in meditation.

These exercises guide your thoughts on a pathway towards zen, with ease. For advanced practitioners going through a crisis, they retrain your brain back to a logical and calm way of thinking. Like anything, your meditation muscle will grow with time. If your meditation muscle was lost in the crisis, it is now time to build it back up!

When you're in a safe place, practice the art of detachment to your crisis through this meditative exercise.

Exercise:

Before you begin, connect to your breath. This is both to remind yourself of the present moment and a biological way to calm your nervous system.

Slow your breathing.

Take deep inhalations and exhalations - go deeper than you ever have before. Take as many as you need until you start to feel connected to both your breath and this moment.

Then, try taking another extra deep breath in and an extra deep breath out. Do each 3 times for a total of 3 breaths in and out.

Now, imagine your conscious mind (or whatever you would like to call the voice in your head, your internal dialogue) hovering above your body. See your conscious mind hovering and elevating above your body. From here, your conscious mind can view your body and the crisis situation as it is down below.

Practice detachment to your body which is currently filled with stress. Observe that you are the observer of your body filled with stress. You are not your body filled with stress. The stress is down there and you are up here, hovering above it.

Leave the stress suit you're wearing, leave the furrowed brow, leave the beaten down body, leave the sadness and fear, leave the pain and hurt, if only for a moment to remember you're fine enough for now, you're breathing and you're detached.

In this removed state, you are free from feelings and cloudiness of judgment. It is here that you can see the situation objectively and are able to make fair assessments from a safe distance (a social distance, one might say).

From this safe distance you may remark to yourself, "Wow, that is truly terrible for that person down there in the circus... I've never seen anything crazier than this in my life." And maybe you haven't.

You can continue to breathe peacefully because you are removed and simply observing from a state of detachment.

Remember a time when your body down below was filled with another pleasant feeling, perhaps joy. Remind yourself that your body can be filled with any host of emotions and the current feeling and experience is not permanent, even though it may feel like it is. It is not important to force any feeling at this stage. Simply, observe.

We are just beginning to observe instead of being overwhelmed.

This is how you start.

Detachment will save you in the most challenging moments and allow you to shield yourself from further pain, so that you can move onto the next step in the process.

It is a way to get away without getting away. It is a way to get out of your stressed self and enter your always available haven of peace.

If it is your first mediation experience, it may start small. Since you are in a crisis, it will be more difficult, but with practice, as anything, you will be more and more zen. And once you can get zen in a crisis, you can be zen through *anything*.

Spoiler alert: we're still at the beginning of this process, so don't expect too much from yourself at this stage (but also don't allow yourself to be hopeless; keep at it).

You just need to be willing. Be willing to breathe. Be willing to slow your breath. Be willing to step outside and view as an observer and breathe again.

Our biggest takeaway: detachment can give us perspective, and temporary reprieve, when we're overwhelmed.

Rather than being your thoughts and emotions, be the awareness behind them.

ECKHART TOLLE

Assess the truth and the non-truths

In an ideal world, we would now be able to enter a state of peace now that we have 'left the circus.'

But hahaha oh my, no no....

I hate to burst your bubble, but we can't live in a state of disassociation forever. Prolonged disassociation is called denial and can be destructive. Instead, we are using it temporarily as a tool to recover, repair and return to peace FOR REAL.

To begin, let's figure out where we are and what we are dealing with.

First, who are you?

What's the truth?

Maybe you were never zen before the crisis, maybe you were sometimes zen for a moment in yoga class, before you started thinking about chips, or perhaps you were an incognito monk on a mountain, minus the shaved head and the penchant for orange.

Perhaps you used to be a bit cocky thinking that you could enter a state of zen no matter what was happening. Perhaps you had the "I am a drop in an ocean and I am the whole ocean" vibe. You know that level of nirvana that people talk about in meditation? Perhaps you were reaching that level every night - not necessarily living in that state forever, but you got there enough that you thought you were secure in the world and that nothing could shake you.

But then BOOM - the crisis came like a bomb and literally shook your world, maybe shook *the* world. The mushroom cloud is in the air, and everything that you may or may not have built before in terms of resilience, is going to have to be learned from the ground up. This is new terrain and it has new rules. You haven't been to hell before, so how should you know how to get back? In the past you had some trying times but compared to this crisis, those days were just some extra hot days in the Australian-outback. It is similarly hot, but VERY different to hell.

The good news and the bad news is: it DOESN'T MATTER where you were mentally before the crisis. Whichever zen level you were at, everyone gets brought down to the bottom level in a crisis. We're all brought to our knees and have the life force sucked out of us. And we all have to find a way to get up from a dark, stinky place we've never been before. You may have been through some shit before, but a crisis is a whole other ballgame. It throws everything off kilter; your outer circumstances are thrown and your inner world is also chaos.

It changes you, it makes us all feel weak and powerless - but guess what, we're the opposite. In hindsight, the crisis will be the quickest and most effective way to strengthen our zen muscle... but we're getting to that stage.

I am more vulnerable than I thought, but much stronger than I ever imagined.
-Sheryl Sandberg

So let's do what works and get there. This is not an ideal world, this is the real world and we can make it as ideal as possible given the circumstances.

Yes, our goal is peace, our goal is to be zen, but getting to a somewhat temperate point is the most we can fathom at this stage. This is not everyday stuff; this is the tough stuff, so that will suffice for now.

"That'll do pig, that'll do." (Babe)

(That's a quote from the movie Babe - the pig who herds sheep and wins some championship. Carry on...)

This is the stuff that will require a few more levels until we get to that normal level of peace. So let's start small while taking another step to zen. Let's start with detaching another way, perhaps a bit deeper this time, and not shitting our pants. This is a true achievement at this stage, by the way. Let's not waste unnecessary toilet paper in a time like this.

Many yogis and meditation zen gurus tell you to think of yourself as the lotus flower, thriving in the mud and overcoming adversity. And yes, this is the perfect metaphor for coming out of a crisis, but before we can think of yourself as a mighty flower, let's first think of yourself as a robot.

Wait, what happened to the circus?

The circus hasn't gone anywhere, we're just detached now and becoming a robot. This is a reflection of how the crisis can morph.

Stay flexible out there. We're taking the next step.

Stay with me, little grasshopper...

Ok, so a robot? Yes, because flowers get squished (no matter that they can be birthed from mud) and at this stage we're not taking any more chances. Draw some lotus flowers on your robot body if you wish.

From your point of detachment, observe, as a robot would if elevated from a higher point of reference. Yes, you are a detached robot in the clouds. Just imagine it. Don't even pay attention to the circus down below for a moment. Just observe your new robot self.

~Robot mindfulness~

Ommmm beep beep boop.

(Is that ridiculous? Perfect, let the ridiculousness wash over you. It's exactly what we need and is much better for us than the stress.)

Imagine you don't have emotions for a moment. You are now a robot.

If you're cradling a tissue box in one hand and holding this book in another, just set the tissue box down for a moment.

You're a robot now. You're out of the circus. You are detached from the crisis. And now, yes, you are merely an observer of your emotions from afar.

You are a robot. You are able to compute what emotions are, but you don't let them affect you the way a human would.

You include it in your algorithm and calculations, but a computer processor doesn't get upset, now does it?

Excuse me, but my computer has lost its shit before.

Was this when you had too many tabs open and were trying to do too many things at once?

Yes, probably.

So let's take *one thing at a time* and **assess**.

A S S E S S to find the truth.

Yes, this is how it should feel. Remember we're putting space between us and the crisis.

And so why now are we searching for the truth?

It is important to find the truth now because so often we are blindsided with the crisis... it came out from left-field and out of nowhere... and it is only at this stage of our process that we can finally assess what has actually happened. We only just discovered we were in a crisis; we need help.

What happened to get us here... and where are we exactly? Let's get to the bottom of it. Let's make a truth map.

All you remember was going about your regular life and then BAM waking up with this nonsense going on. You only finally realized that the nonsense was indeed of the 'epic gongshow' variety. At first glance you hoped it was just a shitty Tuesday, but ney, ney.

So let's take a look down below at the circus from our robot body. Let's start from where we are and see things for what they are so we can make accurate next steps.

You already left the circus temporarily so you can suss out what sort of circus we are dealing with.

You now have a robot's body. Fantastic.

From this safe place, assess what exactly is happening.

See things as they are, but not worse than they are. Meditation helps to center yourself but you don't need to be sitting with your thumb and index fingers together, wearing a loincloth and levitating to see the truths from the non-truths. You can be a robot in the clouds above a circus.

Where and what are we dealing with? Observe from your robot body.

What has happened and what is the trending data? Who are the people involved? What have been their observed actions thus far? What are the perceived true intentions for their actions? What is the expected result based on the current happenings? What are your current options? What outcomes can be deduced from those options? Is there any other pertinent information you're picking up?

Remember, you are a robot. You can see heightened emotions and name them but you don't engage with them. You don't feel them. You are now just a robot up in the clouds! You don't have a heart or a mind; you have a calculating processor for survival.

You are just analyzing the situation for what it is so that you can see the truth of it. This stage is all about being practical and figuring out what is going on so you can move onto the next stage.

This is not how to be zen on a clear day, sitting under a tree with a gentle breeze coming from the east, blowing through your freshly shaved head. No, this is how you survive and thrive by assessing the reality of the crisis and clearing the way through practical steps to reach a point of calm.

Exercise:

Take 3 deep breaths in and 3 deep breaths out.

Let's locate the truths.

What do you need to know from the situation?

Write it down.

You are a robot and these are just circus facts. How many lions are we dealing with? Who are the clowns? Is the circus at capacity? Sit with it until you have enough data.

Once you have a generalized map of what is happening, we can proceed.

Our biggest takeaway: see the situation for what it is.

> **❝**
>
> ... Evaluate or assess the situation, gather the good things in sight, abandon the bad, clear your mind, and move on. Focus on the positive. Stay in control, and never panic.
>
> ―――――――――――――
>
> MARTHA STEWART

Strategize

From this detached state of analytical thinking from your robot body, let's imagine a loose guide for getting back into the circus tent.

We will be going back into the circus tent with a strategy and a new frame of mind.

First, find the good... that is, find the opportunity. Look for the positive. Of course, this may be challenging in a time of crisis, but there are always positives if we open our eyes to see them.

Simultaneously, let's set aside our sob story about woe is me. Yes, you may 'deserve' a sob story, but let's instead write a hero's journey. Yes, it is a crisis - meaning it's serious. Yes, your normal life has been ripped away from you in some capacity. These are all facts, but there are also other positive facts.

For example, if you are living in the time of a pandemic where you are forced to self-isolate to stop spreading a deadly virus, you may think your life is over.

You. Are. Fine.

I mean, you may be asymptomatic or symptomatic from Covid-19 but I mean you are fine.

You are fine enough to be reading. Pat yourself on the back and try to hold in a cough.

The point is, you may miss going out and socializing as much as you used to, you may simply miss going shopping or attending sports events, you may even miss going to the gym (if you were one of the people who actually used their membership). You may miss yoga studios, eating a nice meal at a restaurant without restrictions, you may even miss eating an average meal at a subpar hole in the wall. You may miss seeing your extended family without worrying if you're going to kill grandma by breathing near her.

Maybe you've seen a little too much of your family within your four walls. Maybe your significant other has atrocious farts that are threatening to asphyxiate you. Maybe you're deliriously lonely and wish you could just go on some bad coffee dates in public again, without wondering if that first date is worth potentially catching a deadly virus for. Maybe you miss getting your hair waxed - maybe you now are sporting a unibrow. Maybe you used to get cosmetic lip injections and now your lips look like a deflated fish. But let's abandon the bad. What is good to gather?

In a global health crisis where there is a self imposed or government lockdown, you are now free to stay at home. A large number of people either transitioned to working from home or lost their job entirely during the pandemic. As a result, some people now have a wide open door to the entrepreneurship dream they always aspired to. Some were chronic plan cancellers loving their anti-social nature in full bloom. Some were just tired and wanted to chill - self care anyone? Some people wanted to retire and putter in their garden. Some people wanted more time to read the stack of books waiting on their nightstand or their kindle. Some people wanted more time in the day to get ripped and jacked. Some people wanted the time to cook more intricate recipes. Some people wanted the time to connect deeper with their families. Some people needed time for introspection. Some people wanted the time to finish writing a book and finally had no more excuses for not publishing it...

Guess what? We have the time now. Let's use this moment to consider a strategy for using this situation to the best of our ability.

The crisis can come in many forms and so the path of opportunity has a million avenues - let's strategize.

Exercise:

Take 3 deep breaths in and 3 deep breaths out.

Let's strategize and find the positives from this situation.

What opportunity is there for us? What good things can we gather from this? Is it perhaps, in a strange twist, an opportunity or a call to do something we've been meaning to do all along?

Open your mind and sit with the question. Let possibilities flood your way. Perhaps it is just a tiny whisper of what if I ___? Go with your gut. You will know what to do.

Come up with a strategy for dealing with the crisis. It won't be perfect, but do the best you can given the circumstances. Play out the situations from a detached state for the purpose of strategy.

It is important not to attach yourself too rigidly to this plan or use it as a life raft. It is not the be all and end all. We can't predict the future and we're not trying to.

Once you've really taken some time to sit with this, it is a good idea to write your strategy down.

We are not clinging to *answers* during this stage; we are going to *explore opportunities*, then see how it goes. Perhaps what works will be a combination of things you have conjured up. Likely, the strategy will evolve many, many times.

It is not the strongest of the species that survives, nor the most intelligent that survives. It is the one that is the most adaptable to change.
-Charles Darwin

You may want to know exactly what is coming ahead and make a detailed plan to navigate the territory, but more often than not, there's curve balls. And if you plan for curve balls, then you'll get other kinds of curveballs (that may be straight when you are going left). If you plan for straight balls, then you get molten lava. If you plan for molten lava… you get the point.

We do want to prepare for the circus arena as much as we can, but we need to accept that it is just a process and we need to keep our strategy flexible. We won't freak out later when things don't go as planned because we knew that anyway. We are flowing. We are flowing with the circus stream and not against it.

Notice that the stiffest tree is most easily cracked, while the bamboo or willow survives by bending with the wind.
-Bruce lee

Knowing and understanding that things will change, stay flexible.

The benefit of strategizing is now you have created a pathway in your brain for solutions.

This gives you a strategy and it also helps because it takes your mind away from paralyzing terror.

You have now programmed yourself to go against the panic of yesterday, and this will allow you to come up with a better method of action in every moment to come, had you not been problem-solving before.

You are no longer hopeless because you've brainstormed, and this has tricked your brain into being rewired for success. You've now created a neural pathway to open your eyes to the light at the end of the tunnel.

Our biggest takeaway: strategize and search for the positives.

> ❝
>
> The Chinese use two brush strokes to write the word 'crisis.' One brush stroke stands for danger; the other for opportunity. In a crisis, be aware of the danger – but recognize the opportunity.
>
> JOHN F. KENNEDY

Anxiety is not the answer

There is a myth out there that says you have to mull over it until you get the perfect answer to your problem. EEEHHHH. Wrong.

Perhaps you've tried to mull it over until the magical answer appears. Perhaps you then analyzed some more about a problem that you have little to no control over, only to tire yourself out before any of those potentials even happened! Mulling will not solve it; it will just stress you out.

Do you over analyze? Have you ever argued that analyzing to an extreme length is beneficial?

There comes a time in every analyzer's life when they must put down their thinking cap and go night night.

Put the thinking cap down. You've done enough.

Thought is good - but only to an extent.

If you have spiralled yourself into a dark hole, you have exceeded your quota. Are you stressed and on edge? Are you clenching your jaw, creating knots in your shoulders or grinding your teeth when you sleep (if you are sleeping, that is)?

Assess the situation enough so that you have turned over enough rocks, but not so much that you are struggling to lift rocks up and are manically searching for more rocks. There are always more rocks to lift, but lifting them all will only hurt us. We need to rest. Anxiety is not the answer.

Continuous, detrimental mulling is unproductive and will only serve to break down your health. You may tell yourself you're still strategizing or assessing the truth, but it is time to move on. Yes, strategy is good to protect yourself and find the best in a situation, but beyond a certain point, that level of stress in your body will send you, or keep you, in a hyper-stress state and your health will suffer. And you need your health.

Nothing is worth losing your health over. If anything, that is the most important thing.

If you just started freaking out that you were freaking out, and you aren't allowed to freak out, because freaking out is bad for your health, let me point out the sometimes forgotten obvious:

THE CRISIS WILL END SOMETIME.

Remember that no matter the crisis situation, no matter what is happening right now, it will resolve itself at some point in time.

Perhaps that moment is not now, perhaps it is not 5 minutes from now, but for sure, with 100% certainty, the situation will change and evolve.

Those are just the facts. Life is a constant field of change.

The crisis will end in one way or another.

I know this is hard to fathom in the thick of it.

Wait, so how do you know when you have reached your quota for analyzing and have reached the detrimental mulling stage where you spiral into a dark pit of hellish doom?

You are lying awake in bed, rehashing all that has happened, perhaps there was yelling, maybe there were threats, maybe the news headlines are flashing through your head, maybe it's just a barrage of sorrow and helplessness, perhaps you're going over the strategies of how to protect yourself in the future, what you will do the next day in battle. Which armour will you wear tomorrow?

Put the dumb shit to rest.

You are in bed.

Logically, this is not the time to be rehashing this sort of nonsense (and it is nonsense). If you have battles to be fought tomorrow, then fight them tomorrow with a clear head. If things were said to you, DON'T say them again to yourself. If you got bad news that you are tossing around in your head and spinning propaganda that would make Putin jealous, please, set the news aside. So many times we experience bad things and then replay them again and again in our heads, compounding this one bad experience into many times of traumatisation. Staying up all night stressing about it won't help you.

LET. IT. GO.

It may have happened once but let's not repeat the trauma and create a neural pathway for repeated pain. You don't want to pave that road to trauma.

You are in bed. You are in your sheets. You are lucky and blessed. Embrace your pillow-y softness. You are privileged more than you accept and acknowledge. Realize this. Let it rest. Let yourself rest in this moment and for the next 8 hours.

And maybe your stresses are 'valid.' Perhaps you have every right in the world to be at wit's end. Maybe it is a wonder you haven't had a nervous breakdown - commend yourself for all small acts of bravery and be compassionate with yourself.

But, just because you 'deserve' to feel shitty, should you?

No, obviously not. You would prefer to feel good. You would prefer to sleep at night. You would prefer to lay that nonsense down to rest and have a blissful slumber. You would prefer to activate your parasympathetic nervous system so you can recharge and relax. The first step is to stop focusing on the stupid things. Let yourself sleep.

"But I'm not done assessing," you say. "I'm not done strategizing."

Dear, there's a limit.

Maybe you want to analyze to get the right answer to your crisis, but maybe there *isn't* one right answer. Accept that if there is a right answer, letting your mind rest (at least for a bit) will be the best way to let the answers come to you.

It is very probable that there are many viable answers available to you and no matter which one you choose, you can make it work.

However, your mind needs a place of quiet in order for wisdom to flood in, and if you don't believe that, believe this: go the duck to sleep.

Sleep on it. Your subconscious has your back so let your conscious mind rest.

You've done the best you can so far. You can do better tomorrow. You will do better and better as days on go in this process, maybe not in a linear path but better all the same. We can't change the past, but we can make the best for the future.

And we can do that by going to bed when it's time to sleep.

Our biggest takeaway: go to bed when it's time to rest.

> Some people don't like change, but you need to embrace change if the alternative is disaster.

ELON MUSK

Keep moving forward

Now it's time to wake up and put your game face on.

We are going back into the circus tent. There was a time to remove ourselves from the situation, but the circus goes on, is ever changing and we need to take care of business. You can't leave monkeys alone for too long without getting some sort of monkey business happening.

Remain in your robot body - we will deal with our emotions in a full way once we have secured our safety and taken care of essentials first. Right now is all about survival and making sure we come out on top.

Sometimes going back into battle is not necessarily a physical proximity thing, sometimes it is only going back into the arena with your mind to take care of business.

We took the mental distance to gather our reserves and now we must re-enter the circus tent. It's not like we ever left the circus, we just mentally escaped for a bit and now we must go back. We can't live in denial forever and we need to sort it out.

Whether you are having to correspond in some way with opponents or face the repercussions of a pandemic, this is your battle to fight. The battle will not disappear if you are too afraid to re-enter. In fact, it will get worse. Do not be the ostrich at the circus burying its head in the sand - that is not zen. In order to be truly zen, we must resolve the issues at hand, instead of hide from them. Crises do not fit under rugs, so do not try to sweep them under. Anyway, it will explode in a much larger way if you try.

We don't need to be afraid because we are in a more solid state than we were prior. We don't need to be overwhelmed anymore because we have taken some distance to assess truth from misplaced fear, we have come up with some sort of strategy, we see the positives and we realize the power in analyzing the situation without panic. We also know when to put an end to anxiety, masked as analyzing.

We are able to think of ourselves and the situation objectively, which allows us to embrace our power. You may not feel strong, but know that you are and you are getting even more so with every step. You may not notice it yet because your brain is too busy defending itself, but it will show itself retroactively.

Also, remember to still think of yourself as a robot. Why?

We embrace this robot mindfulness so that even when we are back in the crisis, we are not paralyzed by our emotions.

We know what others are feeling and we can compute it, but it doesn't affect us like it used to.

We may even know we feel stressed, but we are not the stress. We must make certain that we are pragmatic, in a time of great turmoil, so we can survive. After, we can feel, but for now we take the steps necessary to get through this crisis.

Your precise path to zen will look different to someone else's, even if you are experiencing the same crisis.

Exercise:

Take 3 deep breaths in and 3 deep breaths out.

Write down what necessary next steps you must now take to get through the crisis.

What has changed since you last looked around?

Write down the next best thing to do. Remember your next best thing may not be the same thing as someone else's next best thing.

No matter what has happened or what is happening, you can move forward in small and big ways with intention.

You have a map.

Our biggest takeaway: do what you have to do to move forward and through.

> No man is your enemy, no man is your friend, every man is your teacher.

FLORENCE SCOVEL SHINN

Know yourself, know reality, know who you're dealing with

To move forward, we have to also look at who is involved. Perhaps it is not just the situation you are dealing with, but certain people who have made your life a little slice of hell.

Sometimes you are in a situation where the people around you are making you question your own worth, sometimes even your validity. It is also important to keep a clear view of the truth and reality so as not to let anyone distort it with falsehoods. Your robot body needs to assess what doesn't compute!

Exercise:

Take 3 deep breaths in and 3 deep breaths out.

Keep a journal or record of events in a safe place.

Having the events documented can be helpful in more ways than one, but the primary concern now is for you to have your own record of events, in the face of people trying to distort what's happened. You will be firmly rooted in reality. Call it your, 'I'm not crazy, you're crazy' papers. You can use your video recordings or photos of reality when they try to downplay or lie about what happened, either in battle or just to have for yourself. This will give you confidence, so you are not swayed from the truth.

A lot of times in a crisis, the opposition may try to attack your sense of self. Gaslighting is just one of the many psychological attacks you have to guard yourself from. The way to guard yourself is to remember your robot self and remain firm in the truth. Compute only the facts. If it doesn't register, don't keep it in the system. Send it to the trash.

Know who you're dealing with

Acknowledge that if there are toxic people in your life, they will act toxic. It seems simple, but if you want to see the best in other people and hope they will change or are just going through a period of asshole-flirtation…. no! They are fully branded as an asshole.

If someone is repeatedly acting in an unsavoury manner to you and others are noticing (and even commenting on it), yet the person never takes accountability for their bad behaviour, take this as a warning. Take this as a lit up sign advertising their asshole brand.

Imagine them with black marker on their foreheads spelling out "asshole." This will help the next time they try to trick you into thinking their previous assholery was just a phase and that they really, puppy dog face, are on your side, all of a sudden. You want to believe it too. They may shake your hand. They may contort their facial muscles into something that resembles a smile.

You want the crisis to be done and the assholes to be suddenly morally sound and empathetic. Sometimes we want to cling onto a fairy tale. But let's remember our robot body and see the situation for what it is without emotion. You are in a crisis and these people are possibly the reason for it.

Don't take the blue paint and colour over the red person. They are red. They may be trying to paint themselves to be blue and telling you that they are blue, but you have seen them red, through and through, time and again.

Just because you have a heart, doesn't mean they have a heart. And no, them not having a heart is not a challenge that you must undertake to make them grow one. They won't and the energy to endure such an endeavor, when you are already in a crisis, is seriously a waste of energy and misalignment of your mental facilities. It is a losing game. You are trying to survive a crisis. Don't get sucked into a narrative they are spinning.

You can't put a flower in an asshole and make it a vase. We're in a crisis here, not in a flower arranging course.

When people show you who they are, believe them the first time.
-Maya Angelou

Remember that they don't have any say in who you are as a person and how you feel about yourself.

Stand strong. Let the truth ring loudly and consistently. No matter what verbiage they throw at you in their ships of deception, let them sink.

Once you've accepted there are clowns in the circus, it is time to put boundaries in place to protect yourself.

If you can't remove yourself from their presence completely, then make sure to put up a large boundary in your mind.

We don't need to buy into other people's ideas of us or whatever neurosis they are currently dealing with. We also don't need to attend every argument we are invited to.

Surely, they will throw personal attacks at you. See them coming at you like balloons in the air. You can ask yourself the validity of their accusations if this puts their views into perspective, or if you've already acknowledged they are the assholes, just see their asshole balloons either float on by you or mentally pop them.

Pop

A popped balloon does not penetrate the fortress. You are a robot, Don't let them affect how you feel AT ALL. They don't deserve to. If you do let them tear you down, they will be happier than a pig in shit.

If someone is mistreating you, *they* are responsible for their behaviour and YOU are responsible for how and if you continue to show up in their presence.

Our biggest takeaway: maintain a solid sense of self and reality.

Why do you stay in prison when the door is so wide open?

RUMI

Understand it's not personal

Understand that if anyone is against you, it has less to do with you and everything to do with what you represent to them. Nothing is personal to you. In fact, it is personal to them.

Their behaviour says everything about them and nothing about you. It helps to see the asshole as the child they once were. Perhaps they were horribly mistreated as a child and didn't develop true empathy as a result. But no matter what, don't let your understanding of their past let you remove their asshole label on their forehead.

Yes, they are a human but they are still a shitty human that you need to protect yourself from! It is not your job to become their therapist. They don't want help. They want to hurt you. Stop trying to pet the snake when it is ready to bite you.

You are not the snake charmer in this circus, but you can learn about snakes so as to see the whole picture for what it is.

Why?

It will remove some anger from your heart, which is important. You don't need to hate the person/people inflicting pain on you in order to protect yourself. You need boundaries certainly, but anger isn't necessary and will only end up eating away at *you*.

This is your life and you should live it as peacefully as you can and be as full of love as possible.

Our biggest takeaway:
Everything someone says or does is a reflection of them.

I can transform my feelings by being present with them.

GABRIELLE BERNSTEIN

Feel everything

Whenever it's safe, feel. And I mean really feel it all. Get it out.

The circus ends here. We don't need the robot body anymore. We don't need the protective detachment of the circus. It's a crisis and we can call it by its real name.

We don't need to visualize it as a circus lion gnawing on our ankle anymore, when really it may be a health scare, a financial depression, your mother in law, your accident or the lawyer representing the other side.

Goodbye, beep boop beep, farewell.

Our robot shell served us well. It allowed us to both assess the situation accurately and to come back to it with a newfound sense of protection.

Now it's time to embrace it all.

Feel everything that you put aside before. Embrace the feelings you may not have even acknowledged yet, because you were too busy surviving.

Exercise:

Take 3 deep breaths in and 3 deep breaths out.

Embrace all of the feelings you had naturally suppressed during your hyperactive survival mode. Here are some fun emotional release options for you to consider:

The ugly cry
To really achieve full release with the ugly cry, it is important to play music that inspires devastating feelings (try Adele or depressing indie music). Quite often you are already devastated enough to reach the full state, but if you were too used to numbing yourself, get the music to give you a little push.

Screaming into a pillow
Louise Hay recommends punching a pillow - you do you. If you own a punching bag, use it and play angry music (think: death metal or dirty gangster rap).

The whisper scream
When you don't want to alert anyone but want to say AHHHH and act out a scream with your whole body. Pretend you're in a horror film but lost your voice.

The big moan
Moan so loudly that the neighbours wonder if someone is dying or having a really, really good time. This one can be especially fun and is a good way to let out emotions that aren't necessarily attached to sadness or anger. You may make yourself laugh, which is also cathartic.

The sing yell

Sing along to the lyrics of your favourite angry / sad / strong-emotion-of-choice song.

Some people will just want to cry, others may only want to yell, and the rest may want to laugh while crying or any other combinations. You can get creative and do what works best for you. Stay safe and don't harm others, property or yourself. This is all about emotional release and it can be done in safe ways. If you want to throw spaghetti at the kitchen wall, then so be it. Wipe it up afterwards and perhaps may I recommend a rosé sauce?

The point is to feel all your emotions and express them to their full extent.

If you're in a global health pandemic lockdown, and you have the urge to rip your hair out and run naked through the streets, you're going to have to settle for running through your living room in the nude. I hope your cat closes its eyes - there are things you can't unsee.

This experience will allow us to finally release our built-up emotions and perhaps even identify some emotions we didn't know we had. It is important to give yourself the permission and space to fully feel all of your emotions. Don't let yourself skirt by this step. It is crucial.

Deal with your emotions, let them pass through and by you, and then find peace.

Exercise:

Take 3 deep breaths in and 3 deep breaths out.

Now, journal your feelings and takeaways.

List your emotions and write out the possible sources.

Determine if there is another emotion underneath the primary emotion. An example of this is masking sadness with anger, when you've been socialized not to feel sad, or visa versa.

Sit with it. Uncover an emotion at a time as you would lifting a rock from the ocean.

You don't need to feel shame about your emotions, but if shame is one of your emotions then write it down.

Fear is its real name

In stressful situations, underneath whatever else is going on, the core feeling is usually fear. Whether it is fear for your safety or of uncertainty of how the crisis will affect your life going forward, the truth is it all comes down to the primal feeling of fear.

In order to come to a place of peace, we must first acknowledge this fear and all other feelings so we can release them. We must first give the fear its name so we can call it out and send it away.

Sometimes we are so consumed by this anxiety and fear that it feels impossible to move forward in healing. There may be many more emotions that arise later down the road, that we will need to release again - in fact, it's almost a guarantee.

This is why it is important to come back to the moment once you've released the heavy emotions. There might be still stuff going on that you can't control, but it is important to regain your composure, even if only for this moment, so that you can carry on.

It is safe to feel safe.

Remember that you are only ever in this moment and in this moment you are taking in this sentence. You want to be protected. You want to know you're safe. In this moment you are safe enough and calm enough to read this sentence. No matter where you are or what situation you are in, acknowledge that.

We've released our emotions so we are no longer imprisoned by them. We have already done everything we practically can outside. Now we must tend to our safety within.

Safety is created within. What happens later, happens later. We can get to that later. Let's focus on choosing our next feeling which is safety.

Exercise:

Take 3 deep breaths in and 3 deep breaths out.

You have this moment and you can feel safe.

Repeat to yourself that you are safe.

Find your breath. Shake it out. Come back to neutral.

Calm. Breathe. Repeat.

This is how we release.

Our biggest takeaway: it's important to feel and fully release our emotions.

> The human capacity for burden is like bamboo - far more flexible than you'd ever believe at first glance.

— JODI PICOULT

Know it was bound to happen

Life is not supposed to be rosy and perfect all of the time. It is not true that if you are a good person who cares for others that you will never have to go through tough stuff. The reality is that ALL of us, every single one of us, will deal with a crisis of some sort and it is just up to us how we deal with it going forward.

So many of us feel we are being punished, but we aren't. This crisis was part of the deal. This is par for the course of life.

And since it is, dare I say, normal and expected - we can reframe this super crazy situation to be... nothing crazy. And since we are bound to be in a crisis at some stage, why don't we not let it get us down? Or, more likely, not let the crisis get us down for any longer?

Don't let a temporary event or situation become the reason that you give up on yourself or your life. It is a passing event; in the future it may even just be a blip in your life. It may be a big blip or a tiny blip, you may forget about it most days, but if you allow it to pass on its merry way, the blip will make you come out stronger.

This hard time will pass and you don't need to completely fall apart in the process. You may crumble, a bit of crumbling before rebuilding is also par for the course.

"And that's the way the cookie crumbles." (Bruce Almighty)

Strength doesn't simply come about. You don't become a tough cookie out of nowhere. Strength is developed in trying situations. If this is the hardest situation you've ever been through, then you can bet that you will be the strongest you've ever been after it's all over with.

Remember a previous time that you survived. Maybe it wasn't as big and scary as the situation at hand, but at the time it was very challenging. You developed more inner strength because of that event. You handled it effectively. You became so much stronger than you ever imagined.

Or maybe you didn't handle the last mini crisis well - let's say you're the type of person to hold onto your pain. Perhaps you are the type of person to lament about how painful it was, blame others and the situation, and give reasons why you are still holding onto pain, to your own detriment. You have to be willing to let go.

You have to be willing to let go of the situation and the crisis, accept it and not let it affect you anymore. And yes, it is a choice. We will get to more of that later. You can choose to do things differently this time. In fact, you already are.

Your mind is your most valuable commodity. Your mind can either lead you astray or allow you to reach your full level of potential during this process.

Our biggest takeaway: people have survived crises from the dawn of time and you can too.

> In times of pain, when the future is too terrifying to contemplate and the past too painful to remember, I have learned to pay attention to right now. The precise moment I was in was always the only safe place for me.
>
> JULIA CAMERON

One at a time

Crises are tricky things. They love to just surprise you on an average day and shake your whole world upside down. One may call them an inversion junkie, but not in the fun yoga way. For this reason, it is imperative to take it one day at a time.

In fact, it is imperative to take it an hour at a time sometimes - even one moment at a time or one breath at a time - depending on the current severity.

One something at a time.

Ommmmm.

Also, take it one crisis at a time. If you are so lucky to be experiencing what feels like two or more crises at the same time, simply pick your favourite flavour (the most pressing and serious one) and wear your horse blinders for it, for the time being.

Sorry, I already have one crisis. You will have to wait your turn.

Pick the bigger, most urgent crisis and focus on that one. There simply isn't enough energy for more than one at this point. Shelf those others for a better time, once this massive one has settled down.

If you can't shelf an additional crisis because it is pressing and imminent, then re-evaluate which one takes priority at this time. Which crisis takes center stage may change moment to moment. Again, one at a time.

Usually there is a way to get rid of, or set aside, one crisis for a period of time, while dealing with the most pressing crisis. Get creative. Use each moment to really dedicate your energy to what is needed at the time.

In the case of a pandemic, there may be many ramifications of the initial health crisis. Maybe an existing or emerging smaller crisis is also present, set it aside for now. Take care of the important things that are necessary for survival in the present moment and we can get to the others later.

Take it one day and one moment at a time. You have already analyzed the situation, it is now time to live in the moment so that you don't completely lose your mind over things you can't control.

All of your power and control is in the present moment.

Our biggest takeaway: take it one crisis at a time and one day at a time.

> The most precious gift we can offer others is our presence. When mindfulness embraces those we love, they will bloom like flowers.
>
> THICH NHAT HANH

Welcome moral support

The truth is that you CAN survive this alone, but my goodness, it makes it a whole lot easier to have even just one other person in your emotional corner.

If you are someone who is afraid to ask for help, now is the time to get over that. Asking for help doesn't mean you are incapable, weak or a burden. Everyone deserves moral support and you need to accept it in your time of need.

Hug like a koala.

If you are fortunate enough to have loved ones around you for comfort, then take full advantage of your proximity to use the love language of touch. Cuddling and hugging, even a tender pat on the back, can be a great way to release oxytocin, which in turn leaves you both feeling more calm.

Being calm is a place of power.

No hugs, no problem.

If, for whatever reason, you are isolated, there are other ways to access emotional support without physical touch.

Emotional support is fully achievable without ever seeing the person in, well, person. The people giving you emotional support don't necessarily need to be in the nearby vicinity or even the country. Luckily, most of the modern world has access to wifi and every kind of video/voice call feature. Texting can work, but call if you can. It is important to have emotional support as close as possible.

Hierarchy of emotional support:

In person >
video call >
voice call >
messaging >
sending one heartfelt emoji

If all you can send or receive is one heartfelt poop emoji, to show your solidarity with their shitty experience, then so be it. But otherwise, it's best to pick up the phone and communicate like the human you are. Being a robot is *so* last chapter.

Emotional support can look like:
1) A phone call from a loved one, saying they care about you.
2) A kind word from someone in the periphery of your situation.
3) A friend who lends their ear, while also offering helpful practical advice.
4) Any positive reinforcement that supports your journey out of this and reminds you that you will get through it!

It is important to lean on your loved ones during this time, to remind you of the wonderful person you are, and all of the great things that you have to offer in this world. Quite often it is a person's broken spirit that will make them succumb to the crisis, so this is why it is imperative to keep this in check from the beginning.

Why is emotional support important?

Emotional support is EVERYTHING. This will only magnify any confidence of yours that has been chipped away at from the experience. It will also allow you to replenish some of the energy and positivity that was sucked away in such a traumatic event.

This brings us to an important point: do not seek emotional support from those who are incapable or unwilling to give it!

Don't try to hug a porcupine.

Do not reach out to someone who has let you down before, your ex (because you're feeling super desperate) or someone who could be clinically diagnosed as depressed or a narcissist. All of those actions will only make you feel worse.

Take care to choose your emotional support loved ones wisely.

There are also cases where a person is very nice but they don't give the best advice. Some people will weigh you down more than you are already. Make sure to surround yourself with people who have a positive and resilient life philosophy, as their words at this time can either lift you up or push you down further (if you let them). It is up to you to choose who to go to.

The listener
Perhaps you are in the camp of simply wanting an ear and tender heart to listen. You want to vent. You want to be heard. You don't want advice and simply want a shoulder to weep on. In this case, it doesn't really matter if they give good advice or not, but only that you have a quiet space to express yourself. In this case it is important to communicate exactly what you need from them and ask if they are in a place to offer that to you.

Again, choose wisely and don't try to force people to be who they are not. Also, never assume that they know what you need if you haven't communicated it.

The wise advice giver
Perhaps you are craving not only a place to explain your situation but are seeking wise people who have their heads on straight and their hearts in the right place. Venting with no solution is not as good as venting and seeking further advice on the situation at hand. This is a great way to assess other points of view in the interim and open up your eyes to where you may have had a blind spot.

If you need someone who will be quiet and nod, do not go to the person who is more pragmatic and will give you straight-shooting advice that you don't want to hear.

If you need someone to tell it to you straight and help you strategize, don't go to the person who will give you wishy-washy or pessimistic replies.

Know your audience.

During a crisis, you will already be feeling like you're losing your mind, take care not to inadvertently unleash your stress at your makeshift therapist for the hour if they don't say the right thing.

Don't make another crisis. Most likely, that is not really what you are upset about and even if that is what you are upset about, now is not the time to address it.

You have emotional support. It is time to take it for what it is. If you don't like the flavour of emotional support they offer at their ice cream store, then don't go next time. You don't have the time nor energy to change the way they respond or suddenly invent a new flavour of emotional support ice cream. It's not your store. You're the customer. Thank them for their service and never go back if need be.

This is not a time to start a fight with someone because they aren't responding how you want them to. Everyone is who they are and it is your responsibility to engage or disengage in a conversation.

If they're in your inner circle, at best you can communicate your needs peacefully and succinctly. But again, you're going through a crisis so some nitpicking things can wait.

This is a time of crisis; relationship interventions can happen later.

Breaking news: *everyone is also dealing with their own shit.*

Also, please remember, everyone else has their own stuff going on as well. Maybe you are both living out a pandemic together and you both need support. Remember that everyone deals with things differently and wants different things from others. One person may want more space while someone else wants more closeness.

It is best to communicate your needs and be responsive to what others are willing to do. If you are going through a divorce, someone else may be going through a human rights tribunal battle. Also, remember that not everyone announces every little thing that they may be going through at that time. They may have a covert crisis.

If you don't have moral support, or the moral support wasn't exactly what you needed (people are not infallible) then journal.

Exercise:

Take 3 deep breaths in and 3 deep breaths out.

Write yourself a letter, as you would to a loved one, explaining or venting your situation.

Also, write the response letter - aka what you needed to hear from them in their reply.

Accept that no one is in charge of how you feel but yourself. Take responsibility to be your biggest support, no matter what.

It is never too late to make more, or deeper, close relationships and friendships.

Now, if you truly feel you don't have anyone to turn to, it is time to build up your support network.

It is important to remember that support goes both ways and it can be just as helpful for you to lend an ear as it is to need one.

Our biggest takeaway: moral support can hold you up in a tough time.

> Love yourself first, and everything else falls in line. You really have to love yourself to get anything done in this world.

LUCILLE BALL

Take care of your vessel

It is time to visit a place known as Self Care City.

What's that, you can't leave the room you're in? No worries, Self Care City comes to you. We all need to visit Self Care City even on a normal day, but it is absolutely critical during a crisis.

Sleep

It is a bit of a chicken and the egg situation with rest and stress. We must be relaxed enough to sleep and we must sleep enough to be relaxed.

Now, don't go banging your head against a wall. Try for both and hope for one, then go for the next. Do not give up and you will succeed.

The following suggestions will also help to ease you into a restful slumber, by virtue of releasing excess stress energy, or allowing a peaceful state to wash over you.

Meditation

Here are some types of meditation to help you specifically through a crisis, and their practical and very honest implications.

Zen - This one has the name of zen so it must be quite zen mustn't it? It is the ancient Buddhist type of meditation - loin cloth and head shaving optional. If you're in the middle of a crisis, head shaving may already have been a part of your psychotic break, so you already look the part. It is all about just being. If you don't like how you are then this may be quite difficult and you need something, dare I say, more forceful.

Guided - For those whose mind is a crazy monkey and/or they just want to finally let go and be taken for a little ride to destination peace. It is the straitjacket of the meditation world and at the same time, the first class seat in a private jet. It all depends on which one you choose. Guided meditations are a fabulous way to be assisted into both relaxation and sleep. Be sure to choose a guided meditation with a voice you enjoy listening to so it doesn't sound like nails on a chalkboard. Guided meditations can also be written, like the exercises within this book.

Mindful - For those who want to feel they are being zen while also being productive. Ok, that's not the point. Regardless, this is the meditation for busy people and for people who like to achieve. It is easy to check this one off the list and fit it into the schedule. Meditating while sitting on the porcelain throne is an option for this category. You can also mindfully eat snacks or mindfully scratch your ass - all are accepted, as long as you are aware of whatever you're doing in the moment. Just be mindful about it and congratulations, you're doing a form of mindful meditation!

Mantra - You have a quote or affirmation that you want to repeat to yourself so you don't accidentally keep telling yourself the stuff that makes you break down crying. But seriously, affirmations and mantras, are a wonderful way to pick yourself up when surrounded by doom. The messages you tell yourself are important during this time, make sure they support your journey of surviving and thriving.

Loving kindness - This is for those who may be harbouring resentment towards people. You are essentially imaging the nightmare people of your crisis (or any people or all people) as receiving your loving thoughts and energy. If this seems difficult, this is probably the one you should choose. The important thing to realize is, the negative feelings and resentment that you hold towards someone that you have perceived to do you wrong, only hurts yourself. Loving kindness helps you to let go of the negativity so you don't need to grow a second asshole for all of the shit you are holding in your body.

Meditative movement - Meditative movement are other exercises that incorporate mediation or have a meditative effect. The best type of movement one, in my books (oh, look where we are) is yoga. We will get to yoga. It gets its own section. There are also Tai Chi and Qi Gong. Both are great options if yoga or more strenuous exercise is not accessible for you.

Yoga

Oh yoga, you bendy, zen, transformative goddess. You look like an exercise class (you feel like an exercise class) and yet the biggest workout is your mind. Inversion asanas (upside down poses) are transformative as you can see what your crisis looks like standing on your head.

Spoiler alert: it looks bad, but also ridiculous and perhaps that may soften the blow.

Pranayama (breathing exercises)

Breathing is essential for life. We may have found ourselves holding our breath a lot more during a crisis. It may not have even been apparent to you until now or it may become apparent a few days after monitoring your own breathing. We hold our breath or develop shallow breathing during hard times, sometimes we even hyperventilate. Pranayama and breath work can help us. It can remind us to deliver oxygen to our bodies, and to our minds, so we can think clearly. Breath is life and there is no joke about it.

Hydrotherapy and cold immersion

Immersing yourself in water is deeply therapeutic. Whether you have access to an overpriced spa, your shower, bath, a pool, lake or ocean, take the time to use this tried and true tool for rejuvenation.

If you want to take it a step further, make it a cold or cool water immersion. Do you want to scream for another reason other than your crisis and then feel positively rejuvenated? This is what will happen after your body calms down from the cold shock you gave it in the shower. It sounds wild, but it's way better than you can describe. If you can handle a cold shower, you can handle the day ahead.

It also offers a host of other calming and overall health benefits related to increasing circulation in the body. Wim Hof developed a cold immersion method, but you don't have to go extreme here to get the benefits. Simply make your shower cooler, or ice cold, for the last 3 minutes.

Exercise

Exercise is a great way to tire out your body, when your mind can't be stopped. You may be surprised at how much energy you have once you get going or how much easier it is to sleep, once you've tired yourself out.

The body is the last to recover from such a traumatic experience. Your body serves as a memory capsule for all of the pain that you have been through. And stress is the number 1 road to disease, so let's get rid of it through exercise.

It doesn't matter so much what type of exercise it is, as long as it gets your blood pumping and it doesn't create pain in your body. The fantastic thing about the internet is your plethora of options for fitness online.

Dance is an amazing avenue to release stress. It has a wonderful meditative quality and full expression of physical postures. Combined with mood-boosting beats, it can change your state very quickly.

Pick one type of exercise or try them all. Do what works best for you. Some people thrive on what other people can't stand... and some people just stand on their head.

Your body is a temple, not a dumpster fire.

The truth is, we need a clear head for what's happening, what's happened and where we're headed. Do your best to abstain from substances, or any unhealthy coping mechanisms, at this time.

This is the time when you will want to reach for vices and destructive cover ups the most, but you cannot fully embrace your healing without having full and complete awareness. You also run the risk of turning an unnecessary habit into a full-blown addiction. Do your best to live through the crisis as it is and not create another one for yourself.

Be willing to face the hard things as you are. If we face them now, they will be solved. If we run from them and mask them, they will haunt us for a lifetime and create MUCH bigger problems.

No matter what, have compassion for yourself, whether or not you ate an entire tub of ice cream.

Let self-care wash over you.

Over time, you will allow yourself to disengage and fall into your pillow. It may be sudden and quick, it may be gradual or it may be in a non-linear fashion, but you will recover. You will sleep again.

You will find your zen bit by bit, breath by breath.

Our biggest takeaway: self-care is how you repair.

> # Smile.
> # Breathe.
> # Go slowly.
>
> THICH NHAT HANH

Harness your energy

Lingering feelings *will* come up because this has been a shitty time. The road to zen in a crisis doesn't involve a fairy godmother to come along and make all of your stress disappear.

BIPPITY BOPPITY BOO - POOF, all of your anxieties are gone forever.

Unfortunately, that is not the case. You are a human being and are not actually a robot like we were making believe (and that is a good thing).

You went through or are still going through a crisis. Your brain was in overdrive. There will be lingering feelings and it is important we deal with those wisely.

Why? The brain is a series of pathways. If you go down the pathway enough times, it becomes paved. Pave only the roads you want to go down because some destinations do not serve you. This means, when these worrisome or negative thoughts emerge about the crisis, do your best to redirect yourself to something useful.

Yes, you thought you shook it all out, but there was more dust in the rug than you knew. When this other dust emerges, send it on its way, or better yet, use it as fuel.

Fuel for your fire

If you have anger towards injustice, or anxiety towards uncertainty, let this be your fuel.

Anger and anxiety are other words for *unharnessed energy*.

That energy could be what's needed to achieve something great. That energy could be harnessed and have far reaching benefits.

Oftentimes, these crises are great redirectors to a new way of life or even just a side hustle. The spark you've been given through the form of excess anger or anxiety could be expressed through a creative outlet to heal and restore.

How can you use these current feelings to serve you in this process? These feelings can be the driving force of your healing and success. They emerged, so where would you like to put them to good use?

You are free to redirect your energy with this new fuel to go towards something you're passionate about. Perhaps the project you want to work on or your new career path is directly related to the crisis itself. Sometimes, it may be simply a space for you to explore a long time and deep seated desire. It may be in the form of being a champion for women's rights or creating a fund to support women in abusive situations, after you yourself came out of an abusive relationship. It may be starting a fundraiser for a particular disease after a scary diagnosis.

Maybe it is more abstract like creating art or writing poetry that will soothe others and act as an outlet for your pain. It may be simply nurturing your swept aside relationships once you come out of the depths of your crisis. Whichever it is, do what heals you and others.

Use this fuel when you feel it. Don't dwell on what was lost, or what worries remain. Remind yourself of the possible benefits and do your best to work towards them.

The burst of energy that you will get during this time should be harnessed. If you haven't reached this time yet and are still in the thick of things, know the time will come and a window will open for you to use your fuel.

You are not failing because you have lingering feelings, it's all a part of the process.

Sigh, breath and accept that.

Our biggest takeaway: there could be a wonderful outcome to this crisis with your newfound spark.

> Forgiveness means giving up, letting go. It has nothing to do with condoning behavior. It's just letting the whole thing go. We do not have to know HOW to forgive. All we need to do is to be WILLING to forgive.
>
> LOUISE HAY

Forgive all

Forgiveness is essential to survive a crisis because it is an essential element to heal. Perhaps you don't know who to forgive because the crisis seemed to come out of nowhere. Perhaps you don't know who to blame. Perhaps you are blaming everyone. Whatever it is, the person we generally always need to forgive the most is ourselves.

Take the instance of a health pandemic. Perhaps you caught on too late. Well, *everyone* caught on a little too late because too late was after the first case happened and no one knew what was happening yet. Even if you were more on top of the impending doom, you were still behind. Forgive the strange animal that got eaten in China and forgive the man who thought that was a good idea - Pangolin, I forgive thee. Repeat to yourself until you believe it.

We have to forgive ourselves for not being all knowing beings. Perhaps the biggest thing to forgive is that we were ungrateful for our regular life before the crisis began! Perhaps we look back now and realize how absolutely fantastic we had it. Yes, we had struggles, perhaps we even had smaller crises but nothing like we are experiencing now and we feel guilty. We feel guilty for not recognizing the great gifts we were receiving every day... the fresh air, the normalcy. Perhaps we were too busy, trying to do too many things and running ourselves dry. Maybe we were bored and unfulfilled. Perhaps we were going along to get along. Or maybe we knew we had it great but feel guilty we didn't do just a little bit more.

Be willing to forgive yourself. Louise Hay talks about how the willingness is what is necessary, not the act of forgiving itself. This is because by becoming willing, the forgiveness directly follows (swiftly or slowly, but surely). You did your best with the knowledge you had at the time. Even if you didn't do your best and could have done a lot better, even with the knowledge you had at the time, you understand that you can't change the past. You can't change what happened and so it makes no sense to feel bad about it going forward. You know better now so you can do better in the future, and that starts with freeing yourself through forgiveness.

And forgive the assholes and the asshats, yes even those asshats. You don't need to welcome any asshats back into your life after you forgive them but let go of the pain all of the same. Forgive the ones who started the crisis, in your perspective. Forgive the ones who kept it going. Forgive the ones who seem to be making it harder.

A key message to remember is that everyone is going through their own stuff, no matter what is happening or not happening for you. If you're in an OK place, others may not be and visa versa.

Of course, during a global crisis, you can safely assume that everyone will have to come to terms with their own demons (whether passing through a very long period of denial or numbness first).

Forgiveness is releasing yourself from bondage.

Forgiveness extends to even our loved ones during the time of crisis. Never assume that just because you are going through a horrible injury, that someone else is not dealing with a mother in law from hell, is on the brink of a divorce or just lost their home in a fire.

In the case of a pandemic, you can absolutely assume that everyone is going through their own crisis, in their own way, no matter how many funny videos they post on social media. It may not necessarily be a facade, but just not the entire picture. This being said, have some compassion for those people in your life. Some people are handling it much better than others, but that doesn't mean they don't have anything to handle. Forgive them as they are also juggling - yes, they too have their own pandemic eggs and are terrified that one or all will smash to the ground.

~Forgive the ones who start fights and are mean (also create boundaries but forgive them all the same).
~Forgive the ones who can't stop crying because they feel overwhelmed.

~Forgive the ones who make illogical decisions in the face of the fear.
~Forgive the ones who are reverting back to bad habits.
~Forgive the ones who are taking a nihilist approach.
~Forgive the ones who are hiding their pain and not being vulnerable with you.
~Forgive the ones who are self-righteous and condescending.
~Forgive the ones who are trying to control you because they feel they've lost control of their little world - again, boundaries are important, but forgive them.
~Forgive the ones who don't reach out.
~Forgive the ones who have been reaching out a little too much.
~Forgive the ones who shouldn't be reaching out at all.

It is also important here to say that forgiveness doesn't mean what someone is doing is OK, and that by forgiving them or their action, you are condoning it. No, that is not it at all; forgiveness doesn't equal condoning. Forgiveness is acknowledging that what has happened in the past can't be changed. Forgiveness is realizing that wishing it were different and feeling bad that it wasn't different, is a waste of time. Holding a grudge is swallowing poison and hoping your enemy dies. Forgiveness is a gift you give yourself to let go of the pain. Forgiveness is a way to set yourself free from the burdens of the past. No one else even necessarily needs to be notified that they are forgiven because it is for you.

Know this, if someone has done you wrong and you are sitting with bitterness towards them in a dark room, they may be very well just drinking pina coladas on the beach and not thinking of you at all. Stop giving someone power to hurt you in the present when they've already hurt you in the past. Let go so you don't have to relive it. It doesn't hurt them, it hurts you. Free the mental space that was taken up with the bitterness of that experience. Quite often, anyway, we are madder at ourselves for putting up with bad behaviour than we are at the person themselves. Never give anyone the remote control to your feelings. Let go and forgive.

Set your boundaries and then release yourself through forgiveness. You can set boundaries (high as the sky, a fortress that can never be penetrated again) and also be free of resentment of the past.

You are responsible for your life. You can't keep blaming somebody else for your dysfunction.
-Oprah

Our biggest takeaway:
Set boundaries and then set yourself free through forgiveness.

Let go, or be dragged.

ZEN PROVERB

Give up the outcome

Surrender.

Take solace in the fact that the situation could turn out for the worst.

HUH?! Did you read that right?

It may not sound very inspirational at first glance - but yes, take solace in the fact that it could turn out for the worst. That is why you are clouding your mind with worries and panicked "strategies" that turn you into an anxious mess, correct? You are worried that it might be the worst. Well, let's sit with it being the worst for a quick moment.

So what happens when the worst has happened?

Well, here's a revelation, it is already the worst so there is nothing left to panic about. If the absolute worst has happened, then that's it. Boom.

That, right there, is a place of zen.

All the shit that could hit the fan has already hit the fan and now there is no more shit to hit the fan. You can breathe.

There is no will it or won't it. We can SURRENDER because there is literally nothing else to do.

So if you were to simply accept that there is a chance it could turn out horribly and embrace that releasing feeling, you would see that YOU ARE STILL FINE. The interesting thing is usually when you give up your resistance to something, things are more likely to go in your favour, but this is more about regaining your mental state as opposed to controlling outcomes.

You might as well surrender now. Once you accept that there are things out of your control (the external outcome of the crisis, particularly) you can indeed lay your mind to rest.

If it is difficult to surrender, try casting your fear.

Cast your fear onto something else. It doesn't matter if you are religious, trust in the universe, are atheist, agnostic, Catholic, Buddhist, pray to mother Earth or to your refrigerator. This is not a sermon, but it is important for you to cast your fear onto something other than yourself. It is time for you to let go.

Let go and let God... or for others, let go and let refrigerator. The important thing is, let go of the outcome and give it up to something else.

The reason we need to let go of the outcome is for our benefit. Worrying about how this will all unfold, or when it will unfold, or where it will unfold and with whom, will only drive us mad.

We are not psychic. Perhaps you purchased a crystal ball lately and are trying to summon your powers because you are at the last resort. Put the crystal ball down.

It does no good for us to put our energy into worrying about something that we can't control. We've strategized enough, now we must learn to trust that it will all work out OR alternatively, we must trust that stressing about the outcome will only serve to tear us down in the meantime, before our eventual demise.

Exercise:

Take 3 deep breaths in and 3 deep breaths out.

Let it go. Surrender.

Throw your arms in the air and admit that you don't know and that it's FINE.

Why is it fine? Because it can't be any other way and so we are going to accept it.

Put the phone down and stop calling the psychic hotline. Give up the outcome.

Our biggest takeaway: accept that it is what it is.

> Wherever you are in your journey, I hope you, too, will keep encountering challenges. It is a blessing to be able to survive them, to be able to keep putting one foot in front of the other - to be in a position to make the climb up life's mountain, knowing that the summit still lies ahead. And every experience is a valuable teacher.

OPRAH WINFREY

Learn the lesson

Perhaps you had a whopper. Perhaps you got two crises for the price of one. You got a whopper with a side of fries - maybe even a jumbo coke! Maybe you don't remember ordering it, but it's here.

We know what the crisis is and we know the part we played in letting it detrimentally affect us. We have forgiven those involved, including ourselves and we have given up the outcome.

What you're feeling now is the beginning of your peace journey. It has been a long road already and if you're still in the thick of the crisis, you don't know for certain whether you're in the long beginning, middle or almost ending.

Understand that there are some lessons to be gleaned from the crisis experience.

Yes, Yoda, tell me more.

A crisis will come with many lessons. Some lessons are obvious and we learn in the moment. Some lessons are only crystal clear after looking back, but there will be hints along the way if we remain cognizant.

The truth of the matter is that most lessons are difficult to learn. They may be uncomfortable. That is all a part of the learning process - annoying but 'character building.'

A number of lessons may come up for you and it is important that we let each go with grace. While it is OK, and very healthy to feel all of your emotions, there is a point in which we can't keep beating ourselves up. We have to let the lessons go so we can actually repair ourselves and move past the experience.

Exercise:

Take 3 deep breaths in and 3 deep breaths out.

Write down your biggest lessons from this experience so far.

Was your immediate thought, "don't surround yourself with asshats?" That is a good one.

We can glean wisdom from trying situations. You may be too entrenched in it now to realize the significance of the moment, but, in some strange way, brilliance will come of this event. At some point in the future, you will see your strength and resilience that came from this crisis, and how it positively affected your life. You may balk at this, until one fine day, you realize how profound this crisis was for molding you into the remarkable person you became. You may balk until you can't balk anymore.

And that's the thing, many people fall into the trap of thinking this horrible thing happened to them and remain in the hole instead of seeing it for the gift it is. Challenges are in our lives for lessons.

Exercise:

Take 3 deep breaths in and 3 deep breaths out.

Take a moment now to ask yourself what benefit this crisis has given you.

It is important to ask this question once you feel the crisis has passed its peak time. Once the immediate trauma has dissipated, and what's left is you and your mind, that is the time to ask. You can ask it before, but you will gain more insight later on.

What did this crisis give me? What is this crisis giving me right this moment?

For all of us, one of the core lessons is resilience.

It is having the confidence in our resilience. It is knowing we are a person who can get through the worst of it. It is the unyielding stance of a survivor. Now we know what we are not always up against and can make a regular day extraordinary. We can walk through the world as a powerful, wiser person with a second lease on life.

Sometimes perceived hindrances are actually opportunities. The door is shut to the world, but has the window to your inner self opened up?

If you are going through a divorce, are you finally able to embrace your authentic self? If you are going through a sexual harassment trial, are you perhaps being given this experience to assist others through another kind of crisis? If you are seriously ill, are you finally slowing down to embrace your breath? If you had a near death experience, are you suddenly feeling more alive now? If you were betrayed, are you learning the art of forgiveness? If you just lost your job, are you learning to be your own boss? If you just lost a family member, are you learning to find joy in the grief?

Let the lesson go once it's learned.

Getting over a painful experience is much like crossing monkey bars. You have to let go at some point in order to move forward.
-C.S. Lewis

In order to learn the lessons, we have to let them be resolved. The trying time of learning the lesson will end, once the lesson has been learned. Lessons love to greet us with a slap in the face every time we meet them, but they are transitory when we let them pass on their merry way.

Experiences are just experiences. It is what we take from them that matters. Master your mind and reframe everything. We don't have to be a slave to our stimulus. We can be a beacon of peace in a storm. We can come out stronger than ever before. This is your lesson. This is everyone's lesson.

Notice where you may be holding resistance to something. Notice if you are still holding onto your pain of the crisis. If you are not ready to let go then that is fine for now. You can try again in the next moment or tomorrow. When you are ready to move on, you can decide to loosen your grip and then you will let go with ease.

I really do think that any deep crisis is an opportunity to make your life extraordinary in some way.
-Martha Beck

Maybe we are holding onto a lesson and as a result, we keep having to relive it. We keep getting slapped in the face over and over with the same lesson. More than likely, we don't want to be reliving it, but it is a difficult lesson for us to learn.

Perhaps the crisis is long so the lesson gets drawn out. Usually crises feel like forever even if they aren't. It hasn't been proven but I am sure something happens to the space-time continuum to make them seem limitless when they are in fact finite. This is our reminder that our lessons are also finite, if we let them go.

It may be hard to let them go and maybe we don't even realize it is us that needs to let the lessons go, perhaps we think it is the external that needs to change.

This is your reminder that we don't have to experience the same lesson over and over if we truly learn from it. We can step back from the slap before it hits our face. The same potentially painful stimulus will happen in your external world and it will be a test to see if you have truly learned it. If you have, it will pass by. It won't bother you like before. The slap won't reach your face. Why will it pass by? It is because we have already learned the lesson and are no longer attached to it.

An example of this is feeling like you aren't resilient or telling yourself you aren't strong. The lesson is that you are strong. The reality is you are facing and overcoming many hurdles in your crisis. You tell yourself the story that you are weak, despite surviving every day, as a strong person does. That is a clear sign that you need to learn the lesson and let it pass by.

Once you accept your strength, you will see the strength you already have and embrace it more fully. So often we are already incredibly resourceful, even when we tell ourselves we're incapable.

If we know the triggers of the lesson, and are prepared to let it go when the triggers do indeed come (it is a crisis after all), we can let the lesson pass. Letting go of the lesson means not that our external circumstances have changed, but that we have acknowledged it and can send it on its merry way.

The lesson of resilience is the toughest of them all. The very nature of the lesson is to be beaten down until you realize that feeling beaten down will not work for you and deciding to choose another way - choosing to embrace your innate capable self. You can choose to see the slaps coming and get out of the way.

Lessons need to be learned, fine, but what happens in the moment of acute crisis when they're triggered again?

We may have told ourselves the right affirmations, but then we crack again under the pressure. Perhaps, we repeatedly crack under the pressure. The lesson is difficult. The lesson brings up all of the fear again. Perhaps we knew logically what the lesson was, but in the heat of battle, we find ourselves back in our doom's day pattern of negative thinking.

There is a point that you have felt enough pain and are ready to not let it penetrate you anymore. It is not so much a specific time as it is a decision. And it is a decision that you must make ahead of time, before you find yourself in a tough spot again. It is the decision to let the lesson pass. You have experienced it enough times. You have felt all you needed to feel, and known all you needed to know, to move forward. You are ready to get one step closer to being zen.

Let a lesson pass as you would gas, easily, as quietly as you can and then leave the stinkiness behind.

Namaste.

How do we let a lesson pass? Identify it completely and totally. We may be naming something other than its true purpose. The lesson is not necessarily to just learn to self sooth in times of distress. The lesson is not just to deal with your own personal demons this crisis is bringing to light.

The lesson is usually much simpler and the lesson is learning to *let fear go* (or at least not run the show).

Name the fear and let it pass away.

Reword your lesson to be a lesson of fear because every time it always is.

And then the answer is to breathe.

Exercise:

Take 3 deep breaths in and 3 deep breaths out.

Come face to face with the fear beneath the lesson.

Imagine the fear coming toward you again, but this time you don't find it frightening anymore.

You've named it. You've come to terms with it. You're done feeling its effects.

You see the true lesson. You've learned the lesson.

You step back in your power.

Now that we see it for what it is, we can identify the types of situations when it will come up again. In those moments, what will you do next time? When the lesson comes back, what will you say and do, from your new point of power?

And when you're ready, allow the fear to pass by in a little boat into the sky, or in a puff of flatulence, if you prefer.

And you let it go.

Our biggest takeaway: learn what you need to and then let it go.

> The crisis of today is the joke of tomorrow.
>
> H. G. WELLS

Laugh Laugh Laugh

How can you joke at a time like this?! Let me tell you, you need to joke at a time like this - you better joke at a time like this.

This is why humour exists. It is to lighten the dark and make the unlivable, funny. Those who have a natural propensity for humour will find this point much easier than others, but everyone should embrace this healthy coping mechanism.

If you are living through a horror film, are you at least the main character and not just an extra in the background?

Make the villain a caricature. Give yourself a really bizarre superhero outfit.

Lighten up, buttercup. Yes, it is bad but it isn't the worst. You will look back one day and laugh. If you can laugh while still in the midst, you are winning.

Reframe the situation to be hilariously bad and relish in the ridiculousness of it all. Reframe the situation to be funny. You may not be able to laugh now, but try. Try because it works.

If you start by cry-laughing, one day you can work up to laugh-crying... then one day laugh without crying. It's all a process.

This is where dark humour is born and thrives. This is simultaneously where you embrace your lightness.

<u>Exercise:</u>

Take 3 deep breaths in and 3 deep breaths out.

Now, let's get inspired by Laughter Yoga. No, you don't need a yoga mat; for this you only need your face.

Sit or stand in front of a mirror, if you can. This can elevate the experience but isn't necessary.

Now, force yourself to laugh for 3 minutes straight.

At first you won't want to laugh, it may be the first time you have moved your mouth in such a form in a long time and your muscles don't know what to do, but continue on.

Guffaw, giggle, chortle, chuckle and hoot.

Try every type of laugh you can think of, as if you are going to be awarded money for the greater number of laughs you can do. Imagine that you get bonus points for volume.

You may feel silly, uncomfortable or strange, but carry on. Keep laughing and carry on. In fact if you feel silly, lean into the silliness, hard.

When 3 minutes is up, notice if during that time, you started to naturally laugh at yourself.

Repeat the process until you have enough natural laughter bubble up that your body starts to feel itself lighten.

The path to zen is paved with giggles.

If you don't feel like laughing today, you can try again in an hour or tomorrow. But, know this, the more you feel like you don't want to laugh, the more you will benefit from laughing. Give yourself to the process and you will come out on top.

The next best thing is to give yourself to comedic content - whether it be stand-up comedy, a hilarious book or a funny movie. Laugh with friends and family. Laugh at your dog (why is her butt so fluffy?).

Laugh. Laugh. Laugh.

Our biggest takeaway: laughter is the best medicine.

Love
is to people what water
is to plants.

MARIANNE WILLIAMSON

Focus on what matters

Your life may look entirely different than before the crisis. You may in fact look entirely different than before the crisis, but you still matter.

This crisis is like a raging fire, burning away everything that was unnecessary. What's left is remarkable if we let it be.

~Love
~Connection
~Joy
~Health

The rest is a bunch of baloney. No one cares what shoes they wear in a crisis. If you are in a huge crisis, the impractical, fancy shoes are the first to go. Goodbye, crazy high heels. In wartime, people go back to basics. We eat food, we connect with our loved ones and we (try) to get some rest after putting one foot in front of the other, wearing some sensible and comfortable shoes. In fact, you may have traded in your fancy, uncomfortable shoes for slippers.

There are a million trivial little things you previously thought were important that were burned away when you realized they were not essential. You didn't need them. Many of them are social constructs of society or other people's expectations. Many of them are things you bought to make yourself look cool. Maybe it was a motorcycle or something exorbitantly priced because it was a specific brand. Your overpriced purse won't comfort you in a crisis and your motorcycle is not going to hug you either.

In a crisis, no one cares how your fake nails look or the sick rims on your car. The crisis shows us what's truly important in our lives.

Exercise:

Since the crisis, what has been burned away?

Sit with the answers that come, without judging them.

What have you realized matters more now?

Nature, being happy in ourselves, taking care of our mental and physical health, and prioritizing our relationships, are some things that probably came to mind.

Notice how they are all connected to the core values of love, connection and health.

Our biggest takeaway: crises show us what matters.

I have just three things
to teach: simplicity,
patience, compassion.
These three are your
greatest treasures.

LAO TZU

Be patient

Have patience, little grasshopper.

The crisis may be over, or the main part of the crisis may be over, but there are still stress ramifications that can cause inner turmoil. They can be both psychological or even *physical* manifestations of stress.

We must take care to have compassion with ourselves as we ride these waves. The road to embracing our zen, doesn't suddenly leap out and grab hold of us screaming, "I am zen now!!"

You aren't grocery shopping one day and a lady on the loudspeaker announces to all customers, "Attention, you there in aisle four. You have now reached a place of zen and will have no more problems in your life - you get a free box of cookies."

No, day by day, bit by bit, you become more centered, more accepting and firmer in your boundaries of what you will allow. Bit by bit you will notice you are the observer of your experience, other than the experience itself. Bit by bit you will see the beauty in *every* moment, not just in the pictures with filters on.

It starts by trusting the wrong people, eating too much chocolate and feeling guilty for not handling the crisis better. Being more zen arrives more like a whisper, after patiently honouring your experiences, making mistakes, falling back into bad patterns, correcting yourself and forgiving yourself time and time again. It shines through stronger and stronger, when you hear the story you tell yourself when you are interacting with your loved ones. It makes itself known when the crisis is still here, but you are no longer feeling its full weight.

The truth is, you're handling the crisis extremely well already. Your process is what led you here.

You haven't murdered anyone. Well done. You haven't ripped all of the curtains off your windows. You may have drawn the curtains and curled into a ball, but that seemed appropriate given the situation. You only cried a river and not an ocean, and if you did cry an ocean, you didn't drown. Tears are meant to leave the body anyway, so it's good you are rid of them.

Have patience.

This is not an excuse to stay stagnant in a pitty pot, but instead an open invitation to give yourself a big break, because, hello, YOU JUST SURVIVED A CRISIS yesterday and probably will have to survive it again tomorrow.

You are doing so well, even if it doesn't feel like it.

Exercise:

Take 3 deep breaths in and 3 deep breaths out.

Take a moment to just be with yourself as you are.

You may wish the crisis was not letting you down as much as it is, but understand that today you are allowed to feel this way. You will feel this way until you are ready to feel another way.

Accept that you are human and recommit yourself to finding the zen within you, no matter how bumpy the road has been.

Have patience with yourself and understand that journeys out of crises are almost always convoluted and treacherous at times, but they do have an end.

When you are ready to take another step forward, do so.

Our biggest takeaway: be patient with yourself.

> Rock bottom became the solid foundation in which I rebuilt my life.

J.K. ROWLING

Start afresh

How do you want to live your life from here on out?

You can't change yesterday. You can't change even what happened earlier today. What happened in the past is done and we can now move forward. The memories are merely memories.

If the crisis lives on, it doesn't have to live on inside of your head!

Remember that you were given this gift of life and although your crisis has been earth shattering, there are people who have gone on to heal from worse shit than you.

While you are holding this book, solving your crisis, someone is not holding this book, wishing they had it as lucky as you. Pain is pain, when it all comes down to it, but sometimes we need to realize that even with our crisis TRIPLED we are still luckier than most people on this planet, or people in the near or distant past.

Imagine your situation with fresh eyes.

Exercise:

Take 3 deep breaths in and 3 deep breaths out.

Imagine you are a new human being dropped into your skin suit ready for life.

The reason you are dropping yourself in your skin suit afresh is to come into your situation from a fresh perspective.

It is a place of not being limited by the fears of yesterday and the baggage that was holding you back. You're in your new skin suit and you're ready to live this life.

How are you going to choose to live your life?

In a way, you really are a new human. Your cells have a turnover rate to the point that we are becoming new continuously.

The truth is there are a million ways to make your life better. If you gave the same energy that you gave to hating yourself, or your life, to finding the opportunity in your life, then you would have a totally different set of outcomes from the same exact start point.

The world is a wide and wondrous place, and your life can still be beautiful. Be patient with yourself and also realize you are lucky to have this moment.

We have today so let's do something with it. Let's enjoy it. Do we want to use our time to contemplate how everything is meaningless and everything is horrible? That doesn't sound like a wise use of time in our new skin suit. That sounds like a drag.

Use this moment to assess how you would really like your life to look like from a brand new perspective. Maybe the crisis shook up your world so let's ask the question again. How do you want to live your life going forward, accepting that today is how it is and we don't know what the future will hold?

Do you want to be patient with yourself instead of harsh?

Do you want to live more gently?

Do you want to smile instead of stress?

Do you want to be more open to welcoming your zen?

Our biggest takeaway: see your life anew.

> When one door of happiness closes, another opens; but often we look so long at the closed door that we do not see the one which has been opened for us.

HELEN KELLER

Feel the gratitude

Decide to live in gratitude and grow from the experience.

Be grateful for a crisis?! Have you just taken a trip to Banana Land?

At first glance the very thought appears to be crazier than the crisis itself, but the truth is, there are always reasons to be thankful. You just have to pry your sad little eyes open and notice all of the good things you have been ignoring, while the flames of the crisis have been roaring in your face.

Perhaps the crisis has given you an opportunity to get closer to your loved ones. Perhaps getting closer involved a number of tough discussions that needed to happen and you came to a place of love you had never reached prior.

You are now so thankful to have been through the panic and the chaos to reach a new level of intimacy with your loved ones. For a while there, you thought it was at a breaking point, but you now see how indestructible the roots of your relationships are. You're immensely grateful for the experience and each other.

Maybe you haven't solved this area yet, it is likely the crisis has bled into other areas and has caused strain on your loving relationships. Perhaps your loved ones aren't perfect - oh they're not? I guess they're defective and we should return them back to the store. No, we should be grateful for the love they give. No one is perfect.

If they aren't giving much love, ask yourself if you have been in a place to receive it lately. Ask yourself if you have given love to them in a way that they can see it as love (everyone has a love language). If someone is doing their best and is truly in your corner, be grateful for them.

Perhaps the crisis made you grateful for the time to look inward. Yes, maybe you talked to your cat too much and you gave yourself bangs in a moment of panic - but the point is, no one heard your philosophical discussions with Mr. Whiskers, and hats are really in right now. You're grateful for this time because you really know yourself now. You know you're powerful, resilient, vulnerable and zen.

Maybe your crisis made you not yourself in some form. Perhaps you are grateful to take a step back from the hecticness and complacency of your regular life to examine yourself. Maybe you needed the time down in the dumps to spring back up again to a higher level you'd never reached previously.

Maybe you are grateful for making it through such a trying time and still giving it a go. You still did what you had to do. You got through it the best you could. You appreciate the opportunity to witness yourself being an absolute badass in the face of what seemed like insurmountable circumstances.

Maybe something horrendous happened to you, and as a result, you now have deep compassion for others. The crisis humbled you, and you needed to be humbled. You are grateful for the boundless empathy you feel now. The crisis changed you into a more caring person and you are thankful. If you've never felt pain, you can't understand someone else's pain. Now you can empathize with the deepest pain and the most erratic stress.

If you are feeling like throwing your kindle to the floor with the suggestion to be grateful for what the crisis gave you - know that there is still work to do. And that's OK.

In times of crisis, we don't need to beat ourselves up, but instead understand that we are human and it is an unprecedented time. We are doing the best we can at this moment. We can be better in the next moment.

Our brain may still be processing the trauma, but with a commitment to coming out better, and breathing through it, we can be zen.

If we aren't doing the best we can, then why don't we start? If we are doing the best we can, let's keep doing that.

With a commitment to being zen, we will embrace our zen nature sooner rather than later.

Exercise:

Take 3 deep breaths in and 3 deep breaths out.

Make a list right now of 100 things you are grateful for.

If you are knee or even neck deep in a crisis, this will be a bit of a challenge, but no one ever said this was easy. Start small. If you are ready, go big.

Do you have eyeballs or ears to consume this book? Do you have both eyes and ears - wait you have two of each? You are on top.

Our biggest takeaway: gratitude is the doorway to zen.

The point of
power is always in
the present
moment.

LOUISE HAY

Embrace the zen

You've established where you are. You've acknowledged the situation for what it is.

You've detached from the pain in order to see objectively.

You've let the circus play out and watched the lions roar from a safe vantage point.

You've observed the external world and assessed the truth from the non-truths.

You've strategized and stayed flexible to the changing times.

You've opened your mind to pathways for success.

You've put your anxieties in their place and understood where they came from.

You've put one foot in front of another, and that was extraordinary.

You've made the next right decision at the next right time.

You've maintained a solid sense of self and kept a firm grasp on reality.

You've established boundaries to teach people how to treat you. You've also created boundaries in your mind. You won't let anyone tell you who you are or who they think you are supposed to be.

You know who you're dealing with now. You understand that their behaviour had nothing to do with you and everything to do with them.

You've felt your emotions in all their entirety. You freed yourself of their heavy weight. You didn't let them consume you.

You've understood you have what it takes to survive. You acknowledge those moments you've survived before.

You've taken it one moment, one hour, one day, one crisis at a time.

You've focused on what needed focusing on, in each moment.

You took care of business.

You've let yourself be loved by your support system. You've given love in return.

You offered yourself self-love. You've taken responsibility for your own feelings.

You've shown compassion for others and yourself.

You've plunged deep into self-care. You rested when you needed rest. You moved when you needed to move.

You invited meditative experiences into your life. You breathed in hope.

You harnessed your energy and saw lingering feelings for what they were: fuel.

You've forgiven the worst of them and you've forgiven the best of them.

You've forgiven yourself.

You're free from the shackles of the past. You've let it all go.

You've given up the outcome.

You've surrendered to what is and accepted that you don't know all the details of what will be and that's OK.

You've done the inner work, you've seen your own failings and learned the lessons.

You've smiled, when you never thought you would again.

You leaned into your laughter. You conquered the situation by embracing your humour.

You brought light into the darkness.

You've made the best of it. You know what really matters when everything unnecessary has burned away.

You've let the things that needed to burn away go.

You've been patient with yourself and the process to uncover your zen.

You've fallen and gotten back up every time.

You've reverted and elevated again. You're prepared to offer yourself more patience going forward.

You've seen your life through fresh eyes.

You've embraced the opportunity through the pain.

You've decided how you want to live your life.

You've seen how you can help others.

You've felt overwhelming gratitude.

You're resilient.

You're strong.

You've claimed your inner power.

You've striped away the resistance to your peace.

You've done the meditative exercises and you feel more centered. Some days were easier than others, but you're getting better at this.

This is how we have been embracing our zen. At this point, you have either seen the light at the end of the tunnel or you lit that biotch up yourself.

Sometimes you need to take a step back and see how far you've come. You've come a long way. Relish in it.

Take a look around. Where are you? It's a different feeling now, isn't it? It's better. It's lighter. You feel safer. You feel more protected than before. Your mind is a better place to be.

Where you are has less ownership of your mental state.

Whether the crisis is still rising, you are eyeball deep in it or you feel it is in the last act, you are more zen.

Now that you have used these tools to uncover your inner zen, you're able to better see reality from fiction. The lions may still be there, but they're in their cages and you expect them to roar. It doesn't make you flinch so much anymore. Lions do what lions do, and so you keep up your boundaries, and you do what you have to do.

The zen train has not entered my station, yet.

Well, hi, give it a minute. Being zen is an uncovering to your natural, peaceful self, the one that will emerge once the phoenix has burned away. If your phoenix is still burning, let it burn.

You may feel remarkably better already or the process to be zen may need some more time to marinate. If you are still at the peak of your crisis, you will have more processing to do, that is just the reality, but you can be better in little ways as you go along.

How long will it take to get zen? How long will it take to get to the place where time is limitless and defunct? How long does it take to be limitless? What is the time frame for being the feeling that is boundless and unrestricted by time?

The answer is somewhere between no time and infinity.

We've been through enough to know we can make it through some more, no matter the time frame.

We may be tired, beaten down or finally catching our breath. This is a crisis so it will take some time (remarkably little or a lot) for you to bounce back, but when you do, you can embrace your inner zen like you never have before.

The amount of pain you've been through will be directly correlated to your resilience.

No, really. It has been a while and the zen train has not commeth.

The ONLY time you won't embody a zen state is if you are not willing to move on and give up the pain story. Again, have patience.

If you are in the middle of the crisis, part of feeling better is accepting that you are *not* going to feel better for a while. Try it. It is actually relieving. Don't strain to feel good or be zen. Just let yourself be as you are, not necessarily worse, but just as you are. You lose the guilt of needing to feel good and zen, and thereby become closer to it by removing the pressure.

If you have gone through the process, finished the crisis and still don't feel you are moving forward, it could be the result of holding onto the pain.

If that is you, don't let it be you. If something painful happened to you, please let it go instead of reliving it many times over. Try forgiving again, just to see how it feels. Being a victim and holding on to the pain of the crisis, after the healing period is over, is one sure way to stay stuck.

Sometimes we have to choose when the crisis is over.

Nothing will ever be perfect. At a certain point, you have to set the crisis down in your mind. The resolution to your crisis that occurred may not have been the picture perfect answer to what you were looking for. Perhaps it was a silver lining type of situation where you are fired and free, or divorced and free or covid-free and free. The point is, you can now choose to fully embrace a newfound sense of calm.

Sometimes you are not ready to fully heal and move on. You will stop being sad once you've decided you no longer want to feel sad. You will stop feeling defeated once you no longer have a need to feel defeated. You will stop feeling overwhelmed once you learn to let go.

You will start feeling zen when you purchase an orange outfit and sit upon a mountaintop - just kidding, once you're ready to.

And you may feel ready one day and revert back the next. It is your journey and they are not all linear. The important thing is to stay flexible to whatever comes your way, whether from your own emotions or the external world.

It is a crisis and you need to be gentle with yourself, but if the crisis is long gone and you are still living with it within your mind, loosen the grip and decide to let go.

You may have to fight a battle more than once to win it.
-Margaret Thatcher

Never give up on being zen. Anyway, it is a journey and not a one-time destination. Grab yourself a stamp card and come back as much as you can.

Accept that you will find zen once you open yourself to embrace it.

Getting discouraged is a sure-fire way to fail, so why not try again?

Make a decision to survive and thrive and you will. You will not only feel better, but you will feel better than you ever have. Why? You're stronger. You're peaceful and you know you have what it takes to survive the worst of the worst. You have lots to be proud of. You may be tired, but once you've rested, you will look back and not only feel zen, but also immense power and gratitude.

Zen is always waiting for us, on the other side of our fear.

Sometimes the only problem is that we aren't cognizant of the zen already present in our lives. If we see and accept those micro moments of zen, we are able to strengthen our zen muscle.

Micro moments of zen you may not have acknowledged until now:

>It is your unyielding sense of self in the face of trauma.

>It is crying out the pain and then wiping your tears away.

It is taking the steps you need to and doing what's right.

It is speaking the truth, even when your voice quivers.

It is feeling fear but still facing it head on.

It is standing firm in your resolve, even when you're shaking.

It is the resilient impenetrable feeling for a moment, before you go back into battle.

It is the forgiveness you give to set yourself free.

It is the inner boundary of not letting someone's negativity infiltrate your own emotions.

It is the understanding of your own triggers and not buying into them.

It is the commitment to the process when you've failed before.

It is the hope within you that whispers to keep going.

It is the last ounce of energy you need on a tough day.

It is the quiet voice that tells you you'll try again tomorrow.

It is the gentle way you speak to yourself after a challenge.

It is the love you show yourself and others, in all the minutiae.

It is the stillness in your heart, when a storm rages around you.

It is remembering to breathe.

It is the little joke you make, turning a wound into a point of lightness.

It is the shower you take to physically and psychologically wash off the crisis.

It is letting sleep find you.

Acknowledging the moments of zen you already have will welcome more of them into your life.

Exercise:

Take 3 deep breaths in and 3 deep breaths out.

Recall and write down micro moments of zen you have experienced.

They can be as tiny as remembering to take a deep breath in the middle of a battle or a decision to say to yourself, "I won't let this negativity inside."

They can be as tiny as a big sigh after a long day of surviving or a shared smile with a stranger.

Sit with your micro moments of zen and lean into them.

Let the zen expand.

Embrace all of it.

Our biggest takeaway: we've always had moments of zen. We can choose to embrace it fully now.

Just like moons and like suns, With the certainty of tides, Just like hopes springing high, Still I'll rise.

MAYA ANGELOU

Be zen and be zen again

We all know once a new level of peace has arrived.

Sometimes we've been holding it together for so long that we have been holding our breath. It is time to let it out.

Go find your nearest metaphorical mountain top and exclaim to the heavens, "I am willing to be zen now!"

To be zen, you don't have to take an oath of silence.

To be zen, you don't have to renounce your possessions and move to Nepal.

To be zen, you don't have to join a monastery and shave your head.

To be zen, you don't have to be serene as a nun and walk on a cloud.

To be zen, you don't have to chant, say Om or wear wooden jewelry.

To be zen, you don't have to pray to Buddha, Vishnu or sacrifice a goat.

You can be lively, enthusiastic, playful and profoundly powerful… all while embodying a core sense of peace. From that point of peace, you can then make the best decisions and those decisions can make you thrive.

If you want to chant, go for it. If you think you can pull off a loincloth, why not? The point is, it's not essential.

Returning to zen

After weeks, months, hopefully not years or decades, of being in a crisis, our minds can have bad habits of functioning. It is a form of PTSD. We have literally created pathways of anxiety and stress in our brains that became more solid over time.

We may be walking around on a beautiful sunny day, physically free, but our mind may go back to that state of terror, of over-strategizing and replaying the trauma in all of its volumes. We may be afraid that the crisis in some way will return or we're just rehashing it for shits and giggles.

Stop. We can't walk around on a lovely sunny day living in fear of what might happen. Otherwise, what *will* happen is you'll actually ruin the nice day.

It is time to let it go. Find your zen again.

We are not living in denial now or forgetting the past, we are taking the lessons we learned logically but also the peace with it. And there is a lot of peace to be had.

You trust yourself to handle whatever comes and you are at peace in the moment.

Right now you are calm and zen, and that is all that matters. The next moment will be the next moment. You can deal with it then.

You've made your way through the process and graduated to zen mode.

You've been there, you've done that and you've got your t-shirt from Banana Land's gift shop. You've armored up. You've done what you can. You've put in the work and now you can let go of your resistance to being zen.

Let's look at the facts.

You have survived a crisis (holy shit, good for you).

You're still breathing - so what if some of it was hyperventilating, you got oxygen to your necessary bodily functions and that is a success.

Interestingly, when you get zen, somehow the world catches up. The impending doom smoothes out and the urgency dies down. The peace reflects from the inside to the outside. And even if it doesn't, it doesn't matter, because your mind is free and you are no longer consumed with the terror.

You are zen.

Exercise:

Take 3 deep breaths in and 3 deep breaths out.

Sit with this moment. Feel your body and all it's been through.

Feel the fear leaving out your pores.

Feel the peace returning.

Offer yourself compassion and forgiveness.

Offer yourself gratitude for your resilience and commitment to not only surviving the predicament but also thriving.

Place your hands on your heart. Notice it beating.

Feel your life force and energy flow throughout your body.

Know that you are capable, worthy and loved.

Know that your experience will bring great things.

Feel your presence more alive than ever.

See yourself as the still figure in a hurricane.

Breathe and know you're here and you are OK.

Feel the light of your being shining out into the world.

Feel it get brighter and bigger with every breath.

You made it through.

You're zen in this moment.

You can be zen again, anytime.

And the lucky thing is, if it doesn't happen immediately, you get to try again tomorrow. It doesn't happen all in one instant until it does. These are merely the tools to be zen and it is up to you to use them. Like all things, you must not give up.

With every breath you can enter zen mode more fully, every day and in every way.

You're a survivor. You're thriving. You're grateful. You're hydrated (remember to always replenish your fluids after you've cried).

You're zen.

Our biggest takeaway: lay the crisis to rest. Choose to be zen now and again.

> Renew thyself completely each day; do it again, and again, and forever again.

ZEN PROVERB

Acknowledgements

Thank you to my separated shoulder and Covid-19 for moving an unpublished book into the world. I would have done more yoga instead of writing if the damn thing hadn't snapped.

Thank you to my friends and family for being such a strong support network in my time of crisis. Your emotional and moral support meant more to me than I can express. That is certainly my love language and I am endlessly, endlessly, endlessly grateful. Thank you also to the people in my life urging me to be a life/relationship coach over the years.

Thank you to my pets who always instilled a feeling of zen. Too bad they can't read.

Special thanks to my mom and my man for championing me through the writing process and supporting my vision.

I alone cannot change the world, but I can cast a stone across the waters to create many ripples.

MOTHER TERESA

Made in the USA
Middletown, DE
17 September 2020